SANCTITY AND SCANDAL
IN
BEDFORDSHIRE &
BUCKINGHAMSHIRE

A MISCELLANY

by

JOHN HOUGHTON

All Royalties to Willen Hospice and
St. Martin's Church, Fenny Stratford

First published November 2000
by
The Book Castle
12 Church Street
Dunstable
Bedfordshire LU5 4RU

ISBN 1 871199 84 0

Computer typeset by J L Miller, Aldbury, Hertfordshire.
Printed by Antony Rowe Ltd., Chippenham, Wiltshire.

ABOUT THE AUTHOR

John Houghton was born in Eastbourne in 1916. He was ordained in 1940 and celebrated his Diamond Jubilee as a Priest in May, 2000. He began his ministry as Curate in Wolverton (1939–1942) and then served in Northern Rhodesia/Zambia (1942–1973). He worked in Britain for 'Feed the Minds' (1974–1983), retiring in 1983. He lives in Bletchley.

Also by John Houghton:
Borrowed Time Extended
Tales from Milton Keynes
Murders & Mysteries, People & Plots
Eccentrics & Villains, Hauntings & Heroes
Myths & Witches, Puzzles & Politics
Manors & Mayhem, Paupers & Parsons
Historic Figures in the Buckinghamshire Landscape
Twice Upon a Time
They Asked for a Paper
Old Wrinkle Boots

TABLE OF CONTENTS

INTRODUCTION

This books looks at our two neighbouring counties of Beds and Bucks. Through some eight hundred years it touches on some holy places and people in some unholy times. And because times were indeed often unholy it is not surprising that some of the people we encounter were less than holy too. They did, or had done to them, some unholy things even in such holy places as priories, churches and hospices for the elderly and sick.

Religion is the context in which we view the scene. Religion can be, and often has been, compounded of superstition and selfishness. Even when religion purported to uphold law, ways could be found to 'fix' the law, to bend it to gain advantage. We see this happening in the very first pages of the book, as Ailward in Bedford in 1171 is arrested for theft. It is an open and shut case. If found guilty the thief can be mutilated. But wait a minute, says Fulco the Apparitor, if the value of what he stole is less than one shilling, he cannot be mutilated. So they 'fix' the evidence, loading additional items on him which he had not stolen. And Ailward suffered grievously as a result. And that was on the advice of Fulco the Apparitor. And an Apparitor was an official of an Ecclesiastical Court, charged with upholding the law!

Some four hundred years later, also in Bedford, there began a lawsuit which lasted, on and off, for two hundred and five years! It was all to do with the endowments of the Hospital of St. John, which should have been applied for the benefit of St. Paul's Church. Bedford Corporation went to law to secure these. Unfortunately the man they chose as their legal advisor was the Mayor, and he proved to be a 'bent' solicitor, 'skilled in deceit and practised to evade'. When the first hearing of the case ended, the Mayor dishonestly kept all the title deeds and legal documents of the Hospital of St. John. So the litigation to recover them began in 1552 and it only finally petered out in 1760! It was a classic example of post-Reformation plunder.

Religion by derivation means 'the bond between man and God'. But it is interesting to notice other definitions of the word. Napoleon Bonaparte once cynically observed: 'Religion is excellent stuff for keeping common people quiet'. John Wesley once commented: 'Some people have just enough religion to make them uncomfortable'. That witty but cynical priest, Sydney Smith, has left us many epigrams. One of them is: 'What a pity it is that we have no amusements in England but vice and religion'.

John Bunyan's Mr Valiant-for-truth has a healthier attitude: 'My marks and scars I carry with me, to be a witness for me, that I have fought His battle who will now be my rewarder'. So, Bunyan concludes: 'Mr Valiant passed over and the trumpets sounded for him on the other side'.

No such happy outcome befell those who marvelled at the hellfire preaching of the Revd. John Mason, Vicar of Water Stratford in 1692. He confidently predicted that the world would end 'next Whitsun', and that on the dreadful Day of Judgement only those in Water Stratford would be saved. He induced a mass hysteria in the villagers and in all those from elsewhere who had flocked to join them. The story of John Mason's Armageddon in Water Stratford is truly bizarre.

Praed in his long poem called 'The Vicar' has some lines which say:

> 'And when the righteous sects ran mad,
> He held in spite of all his learning
> That if a Man's belief is bad,
> It will not be improved by burning'.

LIST OF ILLUSTRATIONS

Photographs with the initials NK are by Norman Kent.
Those with the initials JH are by the Author.

BIBLIOGRAPHY

Cole:	*Blecheley Diary*
Farrar:	*Old Bedford*
Evans:	*John Bunyan*
Browne Willis:	*History of Buckingham*
Shorter:	*Highways & Byways in Bedfordshire*
Bell:	*Belief in Bedfordshire*
Houghton:	*Myths & Witches, Puzzles & Politics*
Houghton:	*Tales from Milton Keynes*
Houghton:	*Eccentrics & Villains, Hauntings & Heroes*
Roscoe:	*Buckinghamshire*

Chapter One

SINNERS & SAINTS IN BEDFORDSHIRE
SOME HOLY PLACES
AND SOME UNHOLY TIMES

1. AILWARD OF BEDFORD.

In Stephen's 'Criminal Law of England', a report is given of the trial of Ailward of Bedford in 1171. The story is as follows:

'Ailward's neighbour owed Ailward a debt, and when he was asked to pay it, refused, whereupon Ailward in a rage broke open the house of his debtor which his debtor, who had gone to the public house, had left fastened with a lock hanging down outside. Ailward took as security the lock, a whetstone hung from the roof of the house, a gimlet and tools and went away. The children who were playing in the house where they had been locked up by their father, told him how the house had been broken open and how the thief had carried off the things. The father followed him and wresting the whetstone from his hand as he sauntered, wounded his head with it. He then drew his knife, stabbed him through the arm, and taking him to the house into which he had broken, bound him as an open thief, with the stolen goods on him. A crowd collected, one of whom was Fulco, the apparitor, who suggested that as a man cannot be mutilated for stealing under the value of one shilling, the stolen goods should be increased by other goods alleged to be stolen. Accordingly, these were laid by the prisoner, a bundle, a pellium, linen, gowns, and the iron tool commonly called volgonum. Next day he was taken with the aforesaid bundle hung round his neck before one Richard the Sheriff and other knights. Lest, however, in a matter of doubt the sentence should be hurried, judgement was deferred. He was kept for a month in the prison at Bedford. After this it happened that he was taken to

Leighton Buzzard where the magistrates met. There he demanded to fight Fulco, his accuser, or to undergo the ordeal of fire, but with the assent of Fulco . . . he was condemned to the ordeal of water so that he might by no means escape. Thence he was taken back to Bedford where he passed another month in prison. The judges met there and when he was given up to be examined by the ordeal of water he received the melancholy sentence of condemnation and being taken to the place of punishment, his eyes were pulled out and he was mutilated and his members were buried in the earth in the presence of a multitude of people.'

'Ordeal by water' was demanded for a 12th century thief in Bedford. But instead they put out his eyes.

Professor Froude[*], in his account of the martyrdom of St. Thomas of Canterbury, narrates the history of the reputed cure of Ailward in the Church of St. Paul, Bedford, in 1171, the year after Becket's death, as follows:

'While Ailward was in prison a priest, in the interval,

---

[*] Richard Hurrell Froude was Fellow and Tutor of Oriel College, Oxford, in 1827. He was one of the Tractarians who helped to initiate the Oxford Movement seeking to lead the Church of England to recover its Catholic heritage.

counselled him a penance of five floggings each day, and to entrust his cause to the Virgin, and especially to the martyr St. Thomas of Canterbury. At the end of a month Ailward was brought before the justiciars at Leighton Buzzard, where the constable appeared to prosecute, and Ailward had appealed for wager of battle, or for the ordeal of the hot iron. These the judges had refused, and the penalty for felony being loss of eyes and further mutilation, Ailward was delivered to the knife. A neighbour took him into his house and dressed the wounds, which began to heal. On the twelfth night St. Thomas had come to his bedside and told him that if he presented himself the next day, with a candle, at the altar of the Virgin in Bedford Church, and did not doubt in his heart that God was able and willing to cure him, his eyes would be restored. Next day he had told his vision to the dean of St. Paul's Church, Bedford, who had gone with him to the altar of St. Paul's, the townspeople crowding in to witness the promised miracle. There at the altar he prayed and believed. The bandages had been taken from the empty eye-sockets, and in the hollows two small glittering spots the size of birds' eyes could be seen, and Ailward could see. Ailward had gone on Pilgrimage to offer thanks at the shrine of the martyr. Rumours of the miracle had reached the Bishop of London, who had detained him until the truth had been enquired into. The Mayor and Corporation of Bedford had sent witnesses who had deponed to the completeness of the mutilation beyond all doubt.'

Froude appears to have got the story from the writings of Nigellus, a monk of Canterbury, who wrote when Becket's death was fresh in all minds.

2. ROBERT GROSSETESTE OF LINCOLN – 'HAMMER OF THE MONKS'.

In March 1235 Robert Grosseteste was consecrated as Bishop on Lincoln. This huge diocese, with over one thousand, two hundred parishes, came to comprise the Shires of Lincoln, Leicester, Huntingdon, Bedford and Buckingham, plus parts of Hertford. The Bishop was a great ecclesiastic, a great statesman, and one 'mighty in the scriptures'. He set himself to reform abuses in the

Church, especially in the Monasteries. Matthew Paris wrote of him: 'He came down upon the monks like a hammer and was a great persecutor of them'.

On a visitation to Bedford in 1249 he was concerned to deal with disputes between William de Beauchamp and the Priory of Newnham. It is recorded that: 'Euxo, Priest of Caldwell, being accused of many ills by the brethren, and fearing the Bishop's judgement, by the advice of Priors of Dunstable, Newnham, Huntingdon and Bushmead, voluntarily resigned and took refuge in the Cistercian Monastery of Merivale – the Cistercians being exempt from Espiscopal visitation'.

The Bishop died on October 9th, 1253 at Buckden, one of his many Palaces. By his Will he left legacies to a number of Monasteries, including Caldwell Priory.

3. CORPORATION OF BEDFORD V WILLIAMS.

Whatever that dispute had been between William de Beauchamp and the Augustinian Newnham Priory, and however it was handled by the Bishop in 1249, it pales into insignificance compared with the endless and tortuous litigation of a later age concerning the dispute between the Corporation of Bedford and one John Williams, Mayor of Bedford in 1552.

It all had to do with the Parish Church of St. Paul, and the Hospital of St. John with its endowments. The litigation went on and on, literally for centuries. C. F. Farrar in his book 'Old Bedford' tries to untangle it. He wrote: 'Tens of thousands of folio sheets must have been copied for "Corporation of Bedford v Williams". Plaintiffs and Defendents were born into the suit, married into it, and died out of it'.

It was a classic example of how holy places can be caught up in unholy times. As Farrar puts it: 'The post-Reformation period was one of plunder. After the dissolution of the Monasteries followed the dissolution of Chantries. The Hospital of St. John in Bedford with its endowments was scheduled as a Chantry, or "superstitious institution" and in 1547 Edward VI made grant of it to William Staunton for his life, and in 1561 Elizabeth I renewed the grant to John Farnham and his heirs. Thereupon the Bedford

*Seals of the Corporation and
Hospital of St. John*

Corporation, as Patrons of the advowson, alleged that it had never been a Chantry or "superstitious institution"; that its poor brethren were not "religiosi" or monks, but merely almsmen; that it ought not to have been dissolved, and hence the Grant was illegal, and by legal process they got the Grant annulled.'

So far, so good. The Corporation had employed as their legal advisor John Williams, Mayor in 1552. He was a solicitor and evidently a 'bent' one. It was alleged that he, 'skilled in deceit and practiced to evade', kept in his hands all the title deeds and legal documents belonging to the Hospital, and at his death the Corporation sued his widow and sons to recover them, but without success.

But where did the Parish Church of St. Paul come into all this? The Living became vacant in 1599 and the Bishop of Lincoln appointed certain named individuals to be sequestrators of the Living. They were to receive the tithes, rents, profits, etc. of the Parish for the benefit of the next incumbent. But in this they were frustrated by Edward Williams, son of John Williams, the 'bent'

St. Paul's Church, Bedford.

solicitor who had kept in his own hand, and left to his heirs, all the legal documents of the Hospital of St. John.

Enter into the story now the Reverend Andrew Dennys. He was appointed Rector of St. Paul's in 1606. His memorial is in the Church and bears a long Latin inscription. The new Rector sued Edward Williams to try to secure the endowments of the Hospital of St. John which should have been part of the income of St. Paul's Church. In this he failed. As Farrar explains: 'Edward Williams suborned twelve poor men of Bedford, dressed them in antique gowns and paid them 1s per week out of his own pocket, alleging an Order of the Barons of the Exchequer to that effect . . . his object to make it appear that these twelve poor men were

The Rev. Andrew Dennys. Vicar of St. Paul's, 1601–1606. Rector and Master of St. John's Church and Hospital, 1606–1633.

descendents of "religiosi"; that the Hospital had been a "superstitious institution" or Chantry for such, and therefore the original grant to John Farnham was good at Law'.

The dispute continued, through the reigns of James I and Charles I. The Commonwealth under Cromwell came and went. The resumed monarchy of Charles II came in 1660. Through all these periods the dispute still went on! Andrew Dennys fought tirelessly to defeat those who continued to deprive his Living of the St. John endowments. But all in vain. He died, frustrated, in 1633.

But the dispute did not die with him. It continued, on and off, through the rest of the 17th century and well into the 18th century. It only came to an end finally in 1760. So the litigation had lasted inter- mittently from 1552 to June 17th 1760, 208 years!

Who won? And who lost? Old Kaspar, when asked the same questions about the Battle of Blenheim, could only answer:

But what they
fought each other for
I could not well make out.
But everybody said, quoth he,
that 'twas a famous victory'.

4. GILES THORNE.
HE WON IN THE END BUT IT WAS
A COSTLY VICTORY.

The Reverend Giles Thorne was appointed to the Rectory of St. Peter and St. Mary in Bedford in 1629. He was an ardent, and probably intolerant, High Churchman. In 1641 he was taken to Court and accused of 'not praying for the King'. This was surprising. As a High Church man one would have expected him to be quite happy to pray for the King who was Charles I. Perhaps the charge was only made out of spite. A year later further charges were made, based on sermons he had preached which offended the Puritans. He was sent to the Fleet Prison. While he languished there news was given to him that he had been appointed as the Archdeacon of Buckingham. By a bitter-sweet irony, on the very day he received this news, the Puritan-minded Parliament passed an Act proposing that all Archbishops, Bishops, Deans, Canons

St. Mary's, Bedford

and Archdeacons should be abolished!

Poor Giles Thorne, Archdeacon-designate of Buckingham, stayed in prison for five years. He pleaded often for release, particularly because his wife was seriously ill. The authorities relented, but only a little. They allowed him out on bail but only for six weeks. His case would then be reconsidered. By then the Civil War was dividing the whole country and the Puritans were in the ascendant. Parliament set up two Committees. One was 'The Committee for Plundered Ministers'. The other was 'The Committee for Scandalous Ministers'. The very names of these Committees reflect the kaleidoscopic nature of Church life in those troubled times. Which of the two Committees dealt with the case of Giles Thorne is not clear. Either way, he was released on August 23rd 1646.

We lose sight of him for the next thirteen years. When we catch up with him again the year is 1660, the year when the Monarchy was restored. And in that very year everything comes right for Giles Thorne. He is appointed to the Rectory of Merton St. Peter in Bedford; he is instituted at long last as Archdeacon of Buckingham; he is advanced to Doctor of Divinity by the University of Oxford; and he is appointed Chaplain to His Majesty Charles II! So, everything comes to him who waits.

His tomb in St. Mary's, Bedford almost flaunts his belated victories. It says:

'Underneath heare lyes Buried ye Bodie of Giles Thorne,
Doctor of Divinity, Chaplaine in Ordinary to King Charles ye 2nd,
Archdeacon of Buckingham and Rector of St. Marie's
and St. Peter's in Bedford'.

5. JOHN WESLEY. 'THE WORLD IS MY PARISH.'

These words appear on the Tablet unveiled in Westminster Abbey by Dean Stanley in 1876. The memorial honours both John and Charles Wesley. Both were Anglican priests and remained so for the rest of their lives. Their followers subsequently became the Methodist Church.

The inscription, 'The world is my parish' is a quotation from John Wesley's Journal in 1739. The words have a deeper significance than might be supposed. Wesley was ordained in Oxford in 1725. He travelled at once into Buckinghamshire where he preached his first sermon as an ordained Anglican priest in Upper Winchenden Church.

The two Wesley brothers wanted to stir the Church out of the apathy into which it had fallen, but they were frustrated by the opposition of the Bishops and many of the clergy. They travelled extensively all over the country, preaching in the open air because they were denied access to Church pulpits. Many of the clergy resented their casual attitude to the sanctity of parish boundaries and regarded their itinerant preaching as trespass.

John Wesley preached often in Stony Stratford. A tree beneath which he preached is still there, though now it is reduced to little more than a moribund stump. He found Stony Stratford a hard

*This pulpit in Upper
Winchenden Church
was made from one
solid piece of oak.
John Wesley preached
his first sermon from
it after his ordination
in Oxford in 1725.
(NK)*

nut to crack. 'At Stony Stratford. Congregation large and attentive as always', he wrote in his journal, 'yet I fear they received little good, for "they need no repentence".'

He visited Bedford no less than thirty-two times. And on one notable occasion he preached the Assize Sermon before Judge Sir Edward Clive in St. Paul's Church in 1758. His Journal records:

'The Congregation at St. Paul's was very large and attentive. The Judge immediately after the Sermon sent me an invitation to dine with him, but having no time I was obliged to send my excuse, and set out between one and two.'

His travel on horseback year after year is astonishing to contemplate. 'It is true I travel four or five thousand miles in a year', he wrote. It was not unusual for him to ride ninety miles in a day. When he was seventy-one he said, 'Preaching at five in the morning is one of the most healthy exercises in the world'.

He would never have won prizes for horsemanship. His seat on a horse was quite ungainly. He could ride for hours with the reins loose on his horse's neck, while he had a book in his hands.

Wesley's Oak barely survives at Stony Stratford. (NK)

Many of the entries in his Journal are laconic:
'Tuesday, November 11 Preached Millbrook and
Woolton Pillinge.
Wednesday November 12. Preached Bedford.
10 November 1776. Rode from Northampton to Luton.
Preached at Luton and Sundon'.
But sometimes he could be more expansive:
'Wednesday 19 November 1788. I crossed over to Bedford
but where to lodge I did not know; but one met me in the
street and said: " Mr— desired I would go straight to his
house". I did so and found myself in a palace, the best
house by far in the town, where I was entertained not only
with the utmost courtesy, but I believe with sincere
affection. Our room was much crowded in the evening and
pretty well in the morning. There is great reason to hope
that the work of God will go on'.

The Journal breaks off abruptly three days before what proved to be his last visit to Bedford. He was eighty-eight years old and had to be helped into the pulpit and held up there by two men. His end came on March 2nd 1791.

Statistically-minded folk have calculated that he travelled some 250,000 miles on horseback and preached 40,000 sermons. Yet he still found time to write too – not only his Journal, but theological articles and tracts and treatises.

Charles Wesley of course was the great hymn writer. But John Wesley also wrote a few. One of them starts with the verse:

'Put thou thy trust in God,
in duty's path go on;
Walk in his strength with faith and hope,
So shall thy work be done'.

6. TIMOTHY RICHARD MATTHEW.
'LET THE TRUMPET SOUND.'

While Wesley visited Bedford no less than thirty-two times, Bedford had its own home-grown Evangelist too. He was Timothy Richard Matthew. At Cambridge he came under the influence of the great Evangelical divine, Charles Simeon. Matthews was ordained in the Church of England in 1819 and served a curacy at Bolnhurst and Colmworth. By all accounts he was an odd erratic person. Often in the four years of his curacy he would fail to turn up at the church to take a service. And sometimes he would change the times of services at a whim.

He became friendly with a Methodist family named Fielding at Honeydon and married one of their daughters, Ann. He liked what he saw of Methodist religion and began to adopt something of the Class and Prayer Meetings of Methodism. He also began preaching out of doors – 'to sinners perishing in the neglected parishes round about'.

Perhaps not surprisingly his curacy at Colmworth was terminated. He went to assist the evangelical Vicar of Renhold who was Chaplain to the House of Industry in Bedford. (Later it became the Union Workhouse.) The House of Industry had a Chapel and there Matthew preached. He was an excellent preacher

The Reverend Timothy Matthews.

and gained a large personal following.

As he spread his teaching out into the countryside the regular parish clergy became more than a little disturbed. Even the Bishop of Lincoln wanted to know what was going on. He called for a report from Dr Philip Hunt of St. Peter's, Bedford. Dr Hunt reported to the Bishop:

> *'Mr Matthews is (as I hear) a very enthusiastic person, and having married a Methodist, he has latterly, perhaps, become attached to some of their points of discipline; as to Classes, Membership, Prayer Meetings, etc. in so much that he is reported to hold similar meetings . . . Mr Matthews appears to me to be sincere, an enthusiastic person, even fanatical . . . (he might) leave the Church of England to join some other sect of which there is a melancholy variety in this town'.*

Dr Hunt's words proved prophetic. An American arrived from Ohio. He was a self-styled Bishop of his own Primitive Episcopal Church in America. In January 1832 he consecrated Matthew as a fellow Bishop. 'Bishop' Matthews was soon busy setting up congregations over a wide area – in places like Ravensden, North Crawley and Moulsoe.

The Great Ouse at Bedford. (JH)

To say that Matthews liked to blow his own trumpet is not necessarily to accuse him of sinful pride. The fact is that he regularly used a trumpet to collect an audience to hear him preach. (The trumpet survived and was kept later in the Chapel at Ravensden.)

For Matthews the Ouse was his Jordan and he loved to baptise converts in it in the early morning. Matthews died of Typhus in 1845 and was buried at Colmforth where he had once been Curate.

One hopes the Trumpet sounded for him on the other side.

7. THE OTHER FAWKES.
DRAMA AT BEDFORD CASTLE –
TRIAL AT DUNSTABLE.

Everyone knows about Guy Fawkes. He is the man who tried to blow up Parliament in 1605. His infamy has fixed him in our calendar as well as in our memory – each year on November 5th we celebrate Guy Fawkes Night.

But there was an earlier Fawkes, less well known but a remarkable man. This other Fawkes was of special significance to Bedfordshire, but he also loomed large in national affairs. There were periods when he could almost be said to be running the country. Yet he was not an Englishman.

Fawkes de Breauté was born at Poitou in France. He was a professional soldier, ready to serve for anyone who would pay for his services. It was this fact that brought him to England.

King Richard I – the Lionheart – had died. He was succeeded in 1199 by his brother John. King John was soon in trouble. Though an able man, he was erratic and domineering. He lost Normandy, which from the time of William the Conqueror had been ruled as part of the English kingdom; he quarrelled with the Pope; and there were ominous signs that he would soon have trouble with the Barons. That trouble was to culminate in 1215 in the confrontation at Runnymede when John was forced to sign the Magna Carta.

King John relied increasingly on paid soldiers, or mercenaries. Many of these he recruited overseas. Fawkes de Breauté was one

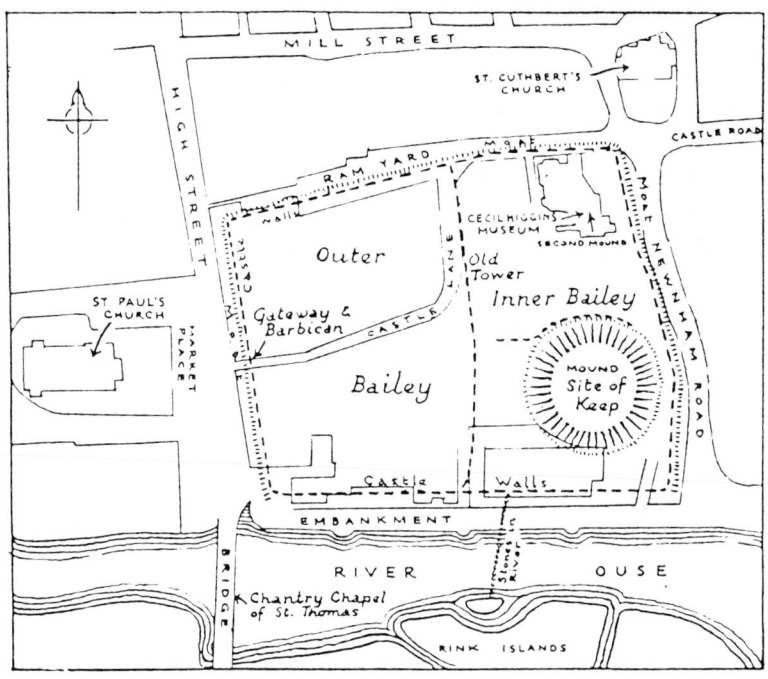

Bedford Castle – where it was and how it might have looked. The 'other' Fawkes was defeated here in 1224.

of them. In his service to King John, Fawkes headed a successful campaign in Wales in 1211.

At the beginning of 1215 the Barons were getting organised, preparing to confront the king. Many of them marched down from the north and linked up with William de Beauchamp at Bedford Castle. The king sent Fawkes to subdue Bedford Castle, which he did successfully on December 2nd 1215. For this Fawkes was rewarded by being given the castle, which he proceeded to enlarge and fortify.

King John increasingly relied on Fawkes and left him in charge in London while he, the king, moved north to subdue the northern barons. That expedition proved ill-starred and King John died.

His son and heir to the throne was the nine year old Henry. A Council of State was appointed to rule on behalf of the boy monarch. On that Council Fawkes served. In military terms his particular command covered all the castles in the midlands, from Oxford across to East Anglia.

In 1217 Fawkes relieved Lincoln Castle, taking William de Beauchamp prisoner in the process. In the same year Fawkes was made Sheriff of Bedfordshire. Thereafter the county became his power base. He already held Bedford Castle. In 1221 he acquired Luton and built a castle there too. To clear a space for the building of that castle Fawkes was ruthless in evicting people from their lands. At least a hundred and fifty people suffered in this way.

Fawkes not only took people's lands, he also deprived others of water, by his construction of his own dam. One result of this was that the mill in Luton, owned by St. Albans Abbey, could no longer grind.

The nine year old Henry grew up. He was to have a long reign as Henry III, from 1216 to 1272. Fawkes continued to serve the young monarch and kept his place in the Council of State. In 1217 and again in 1225 he helped to confirm and implement the clauses of the Magna Carta secured at Runnymede in 1215. So the mercenary soldier born in France had done well in England and was a power in the land – particularly in his adopted county of Bedfordshire.

Perhaps he had become too powerful – too prone to take the law into his own hands. He seemed unable to realise that times had changed. His acts of violence increased. Once he murdered a monk from Warden Abbey. On other occasions he carried off other monks and imprisoned them in Bedford Castle. He continually quarrelled with the monks of St. Albans.

His wife grew alarmed at her husband's behaviour. Her anxiety was increased by a dream and she begged him to desist. To soothe her anxieties Fawkes agreed to mend his ways and even agreed to submit to discipline imposed by the Abbot of St. Albans.

In 1224 judges arrived in Dunstable to look into Fawkes' behaviour. No less than thirty charges were brought against him. He was found guilty of all of them and was heavily fined. Even then Fawkes showed he had not learned his lesson – he seized one of the judges, Henry de Braybrook, and carried him off in chains to Bedford Castle!

All this was too much for King Henry III. He decided it was time to bring Fawkes to heel. He was grateful for the service Fawkes had rendered him during his minority, but he decided he must now trim Fawkes down to size.

So the king came to Bedford in person to lay siege to Bedford Castle. He had summoned Sheriffs from elsewhere and he had collected a considerable force of soldiers, including many skilled in the art of attacking a fortified castle. The Siege of Bedford Castle began.

The outer walls were breached first by the stones hurled at them from the ballista; inner walls were then undermined. Two wooden towers were erected from which archers could fire into the castle. Soon the barbican entrance was breached and the men of Dunstable surged into the outer bailey. They set fire to the corn and hay stored there. The king's men came finally into the inner bailey and the assault on the central tower began.

The garrison of Bedford Castle was commanded by Fawkes' brother. When the central tower finally collapsed the garrison surrendered. Eighty were hanged. Fawkes himself was not taken but he surrendered himself to the king soon after. It might have been expected that he too would be hanged, but he wasn't. No doubt the good service he had rendered in earlier years saved him. He was exiled from the kingdom and died in France soon afterwards.

So died the other Fawkes. He has no day in our calendar to commemorate his exploits, as his later namesake has. Luton Castle is no more. Bedford Castle was ordered to be largely demolished. Some of its stones were recycled for building at Caldwell and Newnham Priories.

Fawkes had first acquired Bedford Castle as a reward for subduing it when it was owned and occupied by William de Beauchamp. Justice was now done to the extent that William was given back what was left of the castle. He was permitted to build a dwelling house there but was forbidden to crenellate it. He lived to a great age and, like the defeated and exiled Fawkes, he too became Sheriff of Bedfordshire.

(This section first appeared in 'Myths and Witches, Puzzles and Politics', by John Houghton.)

8. WHEN LOVE CAME TO CHICKSANDS.

Chicksands Priory in Bedfordshire was founded in 1150 by Countess Rose. It was a Priory for Nuns of the Gilbertine Order, the only House of that Order anywhere in England. It lasted for nearly four hundred years, but in the 1540s, in common with all Abbeys, Monasteries and Priories, it was closed down. Its revenues enriched the crown or were diverted to other projects. Its buildings and lands were disposed of and a succession of new owners made of Chicksands Priory what they wished.

In 1578 Chicksands passed to Richard Osborn, a London grocer. By the time of the Civil War it had become the home of his descendant, Sir Peter Osborne.

Sir Peter was a stalwart Royalist, active on behalf of his king. He was no stay-at-home. His service to the royal cause took him as far as the Channel Islands where he held the Castle on Guernsey for the King. Such loyalty and service cost him dear.

When the war ended in the defeat of the King, Sir Peter was broken both in heart and fortune. But it might have been worse. His wife, Lady Osborne, had relatives on the Parliamentary side, and this fact secured that Sir Peter was able to recover Chicksands, though his lands were much reduced.

Lady Osborne bore her husband twelve children, seven sons and five daughters. Not all survived. Only three sons were alive when the Civil War ended and only one of these, Henry, lived at Chicksands.

Of the daughters, some were married and lived elsewhere. Only Dorothy lived at Chicksands. She was not yet married. At twenty-five she was bright and vivacious. Yet she found life at Chicksands lonely and empty. Her father had become much of a recluse after the war ended and seldom left his room. Her brother was often away from home on business.

So Dorothy was much alone with her memories of the past. And one of those memories was vivid still. It was the memory of the day, four years before, when she had saved her brother's life. It happened on the Isle of Wight. Dorothy and her brother were awaiting ship there to take them to France. Their father, Sir Peter, had retired to St. Malo after leaving Guernsey.

In an idle moment at the Inn, Dorothy's brother used his diamond ring to indulge in a little graffiti. With the diamond he scratched on the window pane a ribald gibe at Colonel Hammond, the Parliamentary Governor of the Isle of Wight. This was foolish in the extreme. To show Royalist sympathies was dangerous; and to insult the Parliamentary Governor in the process further compounded the offence.

When the ribald inscription was discovered a number of people were arrested, Dorothy and her brother among them. They were hailed before the Governor. It soon became clear to Dorothy that her brother would be found guilty and would pay dearly. So she announced to Colonel Hammond that she was the guilty party. This bogus confession saved her brother. Fortunately for her, Colonel Hammond was impressed by her beauty and he was sufficient of a gallant to treat her supposed naughtiness lightly. He contented himself with a reprimand. Dorothy and the others were all released.

That was four years ago. But it had repercussions. An observer of that incident four years before had been a young man named William Temple, freshly down from Cambridge, and about to set out on a tour of the Continent.

William was bowled over by Dorothy's beauty, and full of admiration for her courage in shielding her brother. Dorothy, for her part, was vastly taken by the young man. So romance was in the air.

But the path of true love was not likely to be smooth. Two huge impediments existed. To begin with, Dorothy's father was a prominent Royalist, and one of her brothers had died fighting for the King. William Temple's father, on the other hand, was Sir John Temple, who was a leading Cromwell supporter and had sat in the Long Parliament. He held high office in Ireland and had ambitious plans for his son's future marriage and career.

The second impediment was financial. In the reduced circumstances in which the Osbornes found themselves, there was little prospect of an adequate dowry for Dorothy to take into a marriage. Custom decreed in those days that marriages were arranged and negotiated – they were seldom left to young lovers to settle for themselves.

So the young couple could only wait and hope. They pledged their love to each other and kept their strange courtship secret. They seldom met. Dorothy was alone at Chicksands, where her father still kept to his room. William Temple was in London where he was expected to embark on a diplomatic career. Only letter writing was left to keep the young lovers in touch, and this could only be conducted in secret.

They wrote to each other faithfully every week, and though William's letters to Dorothy have not survived, her letters to him exist to this day, three centuries later.

From Chicksands to London is only about forty miles. There was, of course, no postal service in the 17th century. But every day carriers drove their waggons full of produce, plus a few passengers, from Bedfordshire into the capital. To these carriers Dorothy entrusted her letters to William. They were variously addressed – to tradesmen or lodging-house keepers in London – and from them William would collect them, with a tip or fee to the supposed addresses.

So time passed and the would-be lovers kept in touch. There were others who would have married Dorothy if they could. Ironically one of these was Henry Cromwell, the second son of the great Oliver Cromwell himself.

It amused Dorothy in her letters to William to tell him of these other would-be suitors. She shared with him, too, lots of gossip and jokes, and news of her travels whenever she left Chicksands. But the day when they might at last be joined in marriage seemed as remote as ever.

At last, however, Dorothy's father, Sir Peter Osborne, died. Much now depended on her brother Henry. He had always objected to William Temple, but now he came round and was prepared to sanction Dorothy's marriage to William. The necessary negotiations were completed and Dorothy prepared to leave Chicksands for ever.

She travelled in great excitement to London with Lady Peyton to buy her trousseau. William had already given her his ring. Dorothy and Lady Peyton lodged at first in Drury Lane, but hastily changed their lodging when they discovered someone there with smallpox. Alas, Dorothy soon felt unwell herself and, on November 9th, she too came down with smallpox.

Unlike so many, she recovered. But also like so many, she found that her beauty had gone and the dreaded pock marks disfigured her. But the faithful William had not loved her all these seven years just for her looks alone.

So, on Christmas Day, 1654, Dorothy and William were wed. William went on to a successful diplomatic career with Dorothy at his side. She bore him seven children. So on this happy note our true Chicksands love story ends.

(This section first appeared in 'Myths and Witches, Puzzles and Politics' by John Houghton.)

9. TREVOR HUDDLESTON.
BEDFORD-BORN FIGHTER AGAINST APARTHEID.

Trevor Huddleston was born in Bedford in 1913 and was baptised in St. Paul's Church. An ancestor, Father John Huddleston, was the Restoration Priest who received Charles II into the Roman Church on his death bed, having helped him to escape after Worcester. His father, Sir Ernest Huddleston, served in the Indian Navy and became Director of the Royal Indian Marine.

Trevor Huddleston was an Anglican. He was educated at Lancing and Christ Church, Oxford. He was ordained in 1937 and served a Curacy of three years at St. Mark's, Swindon. It was there that he once said, 'I met and immensely liked the Railwaymen of England'.

Trevor joined the Community of the Resurrection in 1939, taking the three vows of poverty, chastity and obedience. The Community of the Resurrection is an Anglican Order of Monks. It had been founded in 1892 by Bishop Gore in Birmingham. The Community aims to reproduce the life of the early Christians as recorded in the Acts of the Apostles.

In 1943 the Community sent Trevor to South Africa to be Priest-in-charge of its Mission in Sophiatown. In 1949 he was appointed Provincial of the Community in South Africa, and Superintendent of St. Peter's School – 'the Black Eton of South Africa'.

His steadfast battle against apartheid soon brought down on him the wrath of the South African Government. He was persecuted by the police who considered him an agitator. Once when he was taken to Court the Magistrate said to him, 'Is it the function of a Priest to defy the Government?' Father Huddleston replied, 'Is it the function of a Priest to remain silent in the face of injustice?'

In 1956 the Community recalled him to England and made him Master of Novices. He left Africa very reluctantly, but did so out of obedience. In 1960 he was able to return to Africa, though not to South Africa. From 1960 to 1968 he was Bishop of Masasi in Tanzania, East Africa.

He returned to England in 1968 and became Suffragan Bishop of Stepney. He went abroad again in 1978 as Bishop of Mauritius

Trevor Huddleston

Nelson Mandela.

and Archbishop of the Indian Ocean, retiring in 1983.

He never relinquished his opposition to apartheid. In 1983 he became Chairman of the International Fund for Southern Africa. His book, 'Naught For Your Comfort', was published in 1956 and became an instant best-seller. He took the title for the book from a verse by G K Chesterton:

'I tell you naught for your Comfort,

Yea, naught for your desire,
Save that the sky grows darker yet
And the seas rise higher'.

In 1962 he wrote 'God's World', and in 1991, 'Return to South Africa'.

Trevor Huddleston died in 1998. In Bedford, where he was born, a bronze statue to him was erected and in April 2000 his great friend, Nelson Mandela, came to Bedford to speak in his praise and to his memory, and to unveil a new inscription on the Huddleston bronze statue.

The local press reported as follows:

NELSON Mandela told Bedford crowds of the 'indelible impression' Archbishop Trevor Huddleston made on the freedom struggle in South Africa.

'In South Africa we commemorated the passing away of Archbishop Trevor Huddleston', said Mr Mandela, who was locked up for 27 years for his fight against apartheid.

'Many people now claim they were in the forefront of the struggle. Some of these we never knew about. But people inside and outside South Africa would readily admit that Archbishop Huddleston was at the forefront of that battle.

On one occasion, one of our leading liberation fighters was arrested and Father Huddleston said, "Arrest me first". But we needed him to carry on encouraging our people to defy apartheid. Fortunately he obeyed us.

I wanted to pay tribute to one of the greats of the liberation struggle against one of the cruellest ordeals of racial oppression our country had ever seen.

I owe this debt to the anti-apartheid movement and to Father Huddleston in particular. It is a great honour for me to be here to say to him "thank you".'

Chapter Two

WILLIAM COLE
BLETCHLEY'S CLERICAL DIARIST

Clerical diarists are a select company, with Gilbert White and Frances Kilvert among the best known. Not far behind in renown is the Reverend William Cole (1712–1782), Rector of St. Mary's, Bletchley, from 1753 to 1767. He left his Journals in more than one hundred manuscript volumes to the British Museum. He stipulated:

None of them may be inspected or looked at until twenty years after my decease, but all be put up in a large chest or box which I brought out of Portugal, locked and fastened with two iron hoops till that time be expired'.

Given the asperity of some of the passages in the Diary, and the occasional near-libellous entries, that twenty-year embargo may well have been too short. For instance, when King's College wanted to alter the lease of a cottage he had rented, he wrote:

. . . yet after six years the snotty-nosed head of it, soon after his election had the rascality, with Paddon, a dirty wretch and bursar suitable to him, to alter my lease. But from such a scoundrel, and I am warranted to call him no other, with the addition of a liar and mischief-maker through life, no other than dirty treatment can be expected'.

And he could be rude about his bishop too. The county of Buckinghamshire did not become part of the Diocese of Oxford till 1845. So when Cole was Rector of Bletchley his bishop was the Bishop of Lincoln and about him Cole wrote in his Diary:

The clownish carriage and want of behaviour and manners in the present Bishop was so notorious at his last Visitation that everyone was scandalised at it, and among all my Acquaintance I never heard him mentioned but with the utmost Disrespect. Indeed, the Bishop's ungain, awkward splay-footed carriage and Yorkshire dialect is a full indication of his humble Education and mean Extraction'.

The Rev. William Cole, Rector of Bletchley, 1753–67.

He could be scathing too about Fenny Stratford, then part of his parish. He described it in his Diary as 'the sink of all that is bad'. And he dismissed Mr Armstead, the Apothecary of Fenny Stratford as 'the mad and drunken Apothecary of F. Stratford'.

Yet such passages taken alone would give a false picture of William Cole, whose Diary overall shows him to have been a true Pastor to his flock. And not only to those technically his parishioners. Thus, when a farmer in another parish died of smallpox, and none of the neighbouring clergy were willing to bury him for fear of infection, William Cole sent a note to say he would come next day to conduct the burial.

Cole was a Cambridge man both by County and University. He was born in 1714 at Little Abington on the Essex border into a well-to-do family. His parents sent him to Eton where a fellow-student was Horace Walpole. His friendship with that

St. Mary's, Bletchley in the 18th century.

English man of letters, who later succeeded as 4th Earl of Orford, lasted throughout life, nurtured by regular correspondence. Both men were friends of Thomas Gray the poet, and Cole wrote often in his Diary about both of them.

From Eton, Cole went up to King's College, Cambridge, in 1733. By then his enthusiasm for antiquarian research was already established, an interest which he maintained all through his life. His research prompted him to record meticulously a vast amount of detail about innumerable churches. He spent many hours in

College Libraries, saving for posterity much material which might otherwise have been lost. His Diary, too, is an invaluable record of university life as it was lived in the 18th century.

His antiquarian research was almost obsessive. In a letter to Walpole he wrote:

'You will be astonished at the rapidity of my pen when you observe that this folio of 400 pages . . . was completed in 6 weeks'.

His self-imposed discipline enabled him to accomplish some four thousand words and two drawings each day. In another letter to Walpole about his manuscripts he wrote:

'They are my delight, they are my wife and children, they have been in short my whole Employ and Amusement for these twenty or thirty years. And though I really and sincerely think the greatest part of them Stuff and Trash, and deserves no other Treatment than the Fire, yet the collection which I have made towards an History of Cambridgeshire . . . will be of Singular Use to anyone who will have more Patience and Perseverance than I am Master of to put the Material together'.

But that ambition to compile a History of Cambridgeshire was never to be realised. In 1745 Cole was ordained an Anglican Priest. His duties as a clergyman did not impede his antiquariain research and in 1747 he was elected a Fellow of the Society of Antiquaries. But what did stop him from proceeding with his plan for completing a History of Cambridgeshire was an invitation to become Rector of St. Mary's Parish in Bletchley.

The invitation was from a fellow-Antiquarian, Browne Willis, Lord of the Manor of Whaddon. Browne Willis wanted to have a fellow-Antiquary in Bletchley Rectory. Cole accepted the appointment and the effect was to stunt his progress as an antiquary, at least as far as Cambridgeshire was concerned, and it made him a Diarist. As a result, we have:

The Blechely Diary *(his spelling)*

of the

Rev. William Cole

M.A. F.S.A.

Edited from the original MSS

in The British Museum

Tony Watts
(from an old print)

Browne Willis ~
1682 ~1760.

Browne Willis, 1682–1760.

St. Mary's, Bletchley, in 1794.

St. Mary's, Bletchley, restored in 1705–10 by Browne Willis, and by the Victorians in 1868.

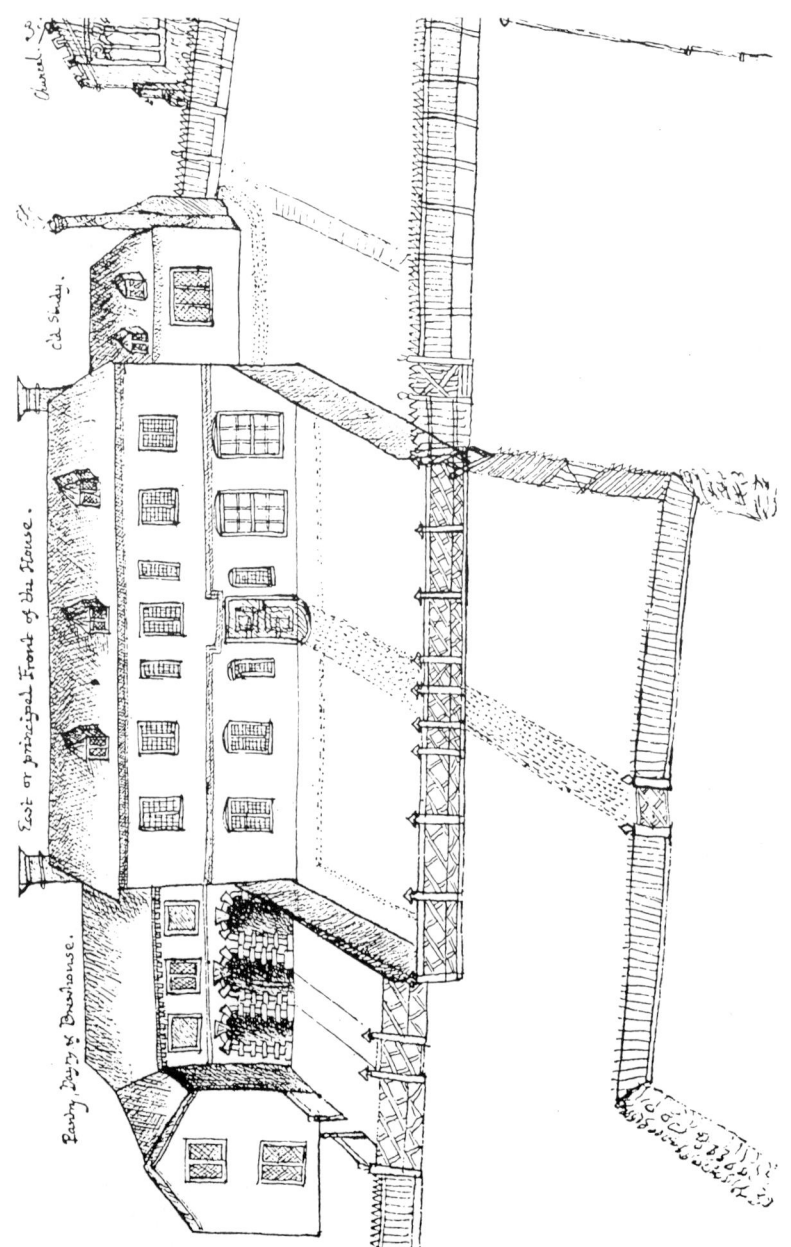

East front of Bletcheley Parsonage. From a pen and ink drawing by Mr Cole, 1765.

Cole was Rector of Bletchley for fourteen years, 1753 to 1767. Few other sections of that prodigious quantity of manuscripts embargoed for twenty years in 'the chest or box I brought out of Portugal' have been published. So we are lucky that at least the 'Blechely' Diary has emerged in print, even though it covers only two of the fourteen years Cole spent in Bletchley.

One can see why Browne Willis wanted Cole in Bletchley. Not only were both men antiquarians – both were the same kind of Anglicans, High Church Tory with marked Catholic sympathies, and with a marked detestation of dissent and nonconformity.

Certainly these two traits are frequently reflected in Cole's Diary:

> *The Discipline of our Church, thro' the practices of the Dissenters, is so relaxed as to come to nothing; there is no parleying with your parishioners in any Point of Doctrine or Discipline; for if you are rigid they will either abstain form all Ordinances, or go over to the Dissenters'.*

Cole was often annoyed when the Bishops seemed to be pre-occupied with what some of them saw as the danger of Papist encroachment. When the Bishop of Lincoln inquired about the number of Papists in Bletchley Parish, Cole wrote angrily in his Diary:

> *Why don't the Bishops enquire after the growth of Dissenters of multifarious Denominations? After Atheists, Deists, and Libertines, surely these are more dangerous to our Constitution and Christianity in General than the Papists whose tenets are Submission to Government and Order'.*

If Cole had lived, say, eighty years later than he did, he would surely have been numbered among the Tractarians in the Oxford Movement of the 1830s when Keble, Pusey and Newman led the revival of the Catholic movement in the Church of England.

All his life Cole numbered Catholic priests among his friends and corresponded with them regularly. When he visited Paris it was in the House of the English Benedictines that he stayed.

When Browne Willis exercised his right of Advowson to appoint Cole to the Living at Bletchley he stipulated that if later on his grandson should be ordained and want the Living for himself, Cole would vacate it. There were those, legal experts among them, and many of his clerical neighbours too, who urged that Cole was not bound by this understanding and could ignore it. But Cole himself felt bound in honour to comply with the known wishes of the now dead Browne Willis. The grandson was indeed ordained and wrote to Cole to say that he intended to take the Bletchley Living and would therefore expect Cole to leave. So on Lady Day 1768 Cole formally resigned the Living and had indeed left Bletchley in the preceding November.

He moved into a rented house at Waterbeech, two miles from Cambridge and found himself living in a parish 'with fanatics of almost all denominations'. He wrote to his friend Fr. Charles Bonaventure Bedingfield:

> *'My finances are miserably reduced by quitting the Living of Bletchley . . . yet I am not disposed to engage myself in any Ecclesiastical matters again. Could I have my books and conveniences about me I should nowhere like better than to finish my days among my countrymen in a conventual manner'.*

In his last years Cole suffered from gout and poor health generally. He died in 1782, aged sixty-eight, with a reputation for eccentricity. To many in Cambridge he was known by the nickname 'Cardinal Cole', a reference to his lifelong leanings towards Catholicism.

He had survived Browne Willis by over twenty years, for Browne Willis had died in 1760. The Lord of the Manor had wanted in the Rectory at Bletchley a man who was both an antiquarian and a High Church Tory priest. Cole had fulfilled both criteria. The relationship between the two men was sometimes less than harmonious. Both were eccentric and both could be cantankerous. Browne Willis had wanted his appointee to work on some of his antiquarian researches and Cole did his best. Willis just before his death had passed to Cole a manuscript in ten folio volumes of his researches in the 'History of the Hundreds of Newport and Cotslow in Buckinghamshire' and asked Cole to prepare them for publication. Cole obliged, completing the transcription, but the book was never published.

'It takes one to know one.' The eccentricities of both men, especially in the matter of apparel, give a good example. Cole in his Diary described Browne Willis's eccentric dress. 'He looked more like a mumping beggar than a gentleman.' And he went on to describe his fifty-five year old greatcoat, his weather-beaten large wig, his old slouched hat more brown than black, and the disreputable footwear which earned Browne Willis the sobriquet 'Old Wrinkle Boots'.

But Cole could dress a little oddly too! Sir John Cullum wrote:

The only time I had the pleasure of seeing him he had as many envelopes as an onion . . . as soon as he unpacked he threw off a rug surtout and entered the parlour invested with a waistcoat, coat, great coat, Master of Arts Gown, and Hussar Cloak, the inferior parts defended with boots, stockings, and galoches'.

The Cole Diary gives us a delightful account of how life was in the Bletchley Parish in the 1760s. Cole was writing at a time when Enclosures were a great talking point, and when the Industrial Revolution was about to begin. He had a keen eye for character and his Diary gives us profiles of so many individuals, a gallery of portraits, of notables both lay and clerical, and of humbler folk too.

Cole could be sardonic and scathing. He frequently confided to his Diary scornful opinions of others, his fellow clergy among them. The neighbouring parish of Stoke Hammond, at the beginning of the 18th century had four incumbents in the space of four years. But then came an incumbent who was Vicar for several decades. He was the Reverend David Timnell and of him Cole wrote in his Diary:

'A worthy and good man, a little inclined to too much laying up of money, yet the effective grippingness of his little wife, Barton, made any defect overlooked. He was disordered in the head which showed itself in his daughter, a good sort of woman, unhappily married to Mr Frank from whom she parted. He was also disordered in the head and they had a daughter who was also thought to suffer from the same affliction'.

One of the most endearing aspects of Cole's character is the human interest he took in gossip, especially gossip concerning some of his fellow clergy! There is no doubt Cole loved a bit of scandal!

> '2nd October 1767. Mr Knapp (Rector of Shenley) told me that Mr Goodwin (Rector of Loughton) was in great affliction on account of their late maidservant who went away about a fortnight ago and has reported that Mr Goodwin offered her five guineas to lie with her, which on her refusal he offered her double to say nothing of it.'

> 'Saturday 3rd October. Mrs Holt (wife of the Lord of the Manor of Little Loughton) told me of Mr Goodwin's offering the maid, soon after she came to them in November, to lie with her; that she at another time gave him a slap in the face and made it black for some time. Mr Goodwin came to dinner but said not a word . . . Mrs Holt said that Mr Goodwin once being in liquor had put his hand under the maid's petti coats . . .'

> '17th October. Mr Eyles (Vicar of Old Bradwell) told me a great deal of scandal of other people and forgot how the world talks of him. (He had a wayward son at Cambridge.) He said Mr Goodwin lay with Mrs Holt and that Mrs G told Frank that her husband lay in the same bed with her for three weeks together but never touched her; that Mr Knapp and his wife lived very unhappily, that they neither spoke to one another or bedded together sometimes for three weeks together; that the widow Woods was a kept mistress and that Mr Pitts (Rector of Great Brickhill) said that none of his neighbours was anything of a scholar or that he could learn anything from other abundance of tittle-tattle. I told him of Mr Pitts' former behaviour to me and his talk to Mrs Willis about my reputation and he seemed delighted with the acquisition.'

Fascinating though the 'Blechely' Diary is, an infinitely greater amount of Cole's outpourings is still only available in manuscript form – a mine of information for scholars able and willing to seek it out. Posterity owes him a debt of gratitude because so much that he recorded longhand in folio form could have disappeared for ever. As it is, the fruit of his research is still there to be harvested for any scholar who seeks access to it. In his manuscripts collection of 'Parochial Antiquities for the County of Bucks' there is a wealth of material on parish churches as they were in the 18th century before the Victorian era would bring in the (sometimes) destructive effects of 'restoration'. Cole was researching and writing of what was still a largely medieval pattern of life in North Bucks., before the effects of enclosures and imminence of industrialisation would bring their inevitable and far-reaching changes.

Meanwhile the reader of the Bletchley Diary can enjoy the word pictures he paints of life in the 1760s in and around Bletchley. He can follow the running dispute Cole waged with that troublesome cleric Ralph Leycester. Cole himself had appointed Leycester to be Parish Priest at St. Martin's Church in Fenny Stratford, an appointment he later bitterly regretted. Leycester proved to be a thorough nuisance. Despite all Cole's complaints to the Bishop of Lincoln and requests to have Leycester trimmed down to size, the Bishop either wouldn't or couldn't oblige. And Leycester lived to have the last word, surviving at Fenny Stratford long after Cole himself had resigned and moved to Cambridge. *(See Chapter Thirteen.)*

But above all there is the evidence that the Diary affords of the faithful pastoral concern of a parish priest who knew his flock and sought to serve it.

The Bletchley Diary ends with the entry for the last day of 1767. By then Cole is installed in his rented cottage at Waterbeech in Cambridge. His servant Tom is still with him, and Bletchley is still much in his mind as he writes:

Thursday Dec. 31. St. Sylvester, Pope. Thank God for his mercies of last year and pray God to prosper me in that to come. Very severe frost. Tom went out a-shooting with Henry and Edward Mason all Day till 5 o'clock when they dined in the Kitchen; they only killed a Wild Duck and a Brace of Teal. Letter from Mr Willis dated at Waterhall to give me Notice he was ordained at Christ's Church on Sunday 20

*and sent me a copy of the Bond by which I am allowed
3 Calendar months after his Notice of 27 of this month.
Yet he wants me to resign directly, and says the People at
Bletchley are uneasy that Service is performed only once a
Day . . . Put up some Books on the shelves upstairs'.*

Chapter Three

CRANKS AND CHARACTERS IN BUCKS

1. WILLIAM DODD.
MACARONI PARSON HANGED AT TYBURN.

It stands to reason that among the many hundreds of rural clergy down the centuries there will have been many who were cranks and characters. And even the occasional crook!

One such was William Dodd. He himself was the son of a country cleric, the Vicar of Bourne in Lincolnshire. William's father hoped that his son would follow him into the church, but young Dodd had other ideas. He wanted to be an author and a playwright. As a scholar at Cambridge he met and fell in love with a girl of sixteen, Mary Perkins. Without telling his father he married her. Learning of this, the Vicar of Bourne took the next coach to London. He persuaded his son not only to give up all ideas of writing for the stage, but also to return to Cambridge to resume his studies and to prepare for ordination.

In October 1751 William Dodd was ordained by the Bishop of Ely and went to serve a curacy in the then country district of West Ham. For the next ten years he made every effort to land a good living. In this he at last succeeded, not once but thrice, for he managed to be appointed Rector of *three* country parishes: Wing, Chalgrave and Hockliffe. He held all three in plurality and took the income from all three, but lived himself in London, paying a pittance to curates to look after the country parishes while the absentee Rector collected the tithes.

There is no doubt about the abilities of William Dodd. He was a Doctor of Divinity, a talented author, and he secured appointment as a Royal Chaplain. He was a popular preacher, preaching 'very eloquently and touchingly' according to Horace Walpole. He built himself a London Chapel in Pimlico. Crowds,

William Dodd,
hanged at Tyburn

including royalty, came to hear him preach. He was popular everywhere, extravagantly dressed and known as 'The Macaroni Parson', macaroni being an 18th century word for a dandy.

One might have supposed that all was going well for the Reverend Dr William Dodd. He had his three rural parishes but could still live and flourish in London. He was universally popular, admired for his preaching and well in with high society. He was the friend and protegé of the Earl of Chesterfield. And he had his Royal Chaplaincy.

But to all this seeming success there was a down side. The fact

Wing Church, one of three held in plurality by William Dodd. (JH)

is that he was living way beyond his means, was heavily in debt
and was being aggressively pursued by his creditors. Foolishly
and desperately he sought a way out of his plight by forgery. He
went to a Stockbroker named Robertson and, claiming to be
acting on behalf of Lord Chesterfield, offered Robertson a Bond
for £4,200. The Bond bore Lord Chesterfield's signature, forged
by Dr Dodd.

The forgery was quickly exposed and on February 22nd 1777
Dr Dodd was put on trial. On May 26th 1777 he was found guilty
and sentenced to be hanged. To await his execution he was kept in
Newgate Gaol and there he was visited by a constant stream of
notable visitors, including John Wesley and Dr Johnson. Some
twenty-three thousand people signed a petition for his release.

After one of his visits to the condemned man John Wesley
said, 'I doubt not, God will bring good out of evil'. And in a sense
he was later proved right. The Dodd affair helped to convince
many that the draconian laws of capital punishment must be
changed. But it took another half century for this to happen.

Meanwhile, in Newgate Dr Dodd fought for his life but came
to realise that only one avenue of escape remained, the possibility

of Royal Clemency. After all, he had held a Royal Chaplaincy. But no Royal Pardon was forthcoming.

One bizarre episode marked his last weeks in Newgate. Dr Dodd preached a sermon to his fellow inmates. What made this bizarre was the fact that the sermon he preached was not his own – it was composed for him by Dr Johnson!

On 27th June 1777 the Reverend Dr William Dodd was taken to Tyburn and was there hanged. He was forty-eight. Also hanged with him was a fifteen year old lad who had stolen two half-crowns and some silver. Evidence came to light later that the desperate William Dodd had made a secret plan whereby he might yet survive his hanging. The plan was that the hangman would cut the rope as quickly as possible after the drop, and friends would rush his body to a surgeon who would resuscitate him. But this plan was frustrated by the sheer size of the crowds who had come to witness the execution and there was nothing any surgeon could do to bring Dodd back to life.

2. JOHN NEWTON.
SLAVE TRADER TURNED PRIEST.

An exact contemporary of Dr William Dodd was another country parson. He was John Newton who for sixteen years was first Curate and then Vicar of Olney. His story far outstrips that of William Dodd for its sheer improbability. For before he became a parson John Newton had for years been a slave trader. Nor was that all. John Newton earned the reputation of being a blasphemous, drunken profligate and the declared enemy of religion!

How did such a man end up as an Anglican country parson? In a way it can be said that he experienced conversion in two

John Newton, the former slave trader, who became vicar of Olney.

instalments. The first occurred while he was still engaged in the slave trade. The ship in which he then served was caught in a violent storm in the Atlantic. Newton spent hours lashed to the wheel trying to keep the ship afloat. That experience led him to believe that his life had been saved for a purpose. From that moment onwards his blasphemy and his mocking of religion ceased. But he certainly didn't turn saint overnight – his drunkenness and foul language continued as before.

But later there came another personal crisis. He married Mary Catlett, his childhood sweetheart and became Captain of his own ship, still involved in the slave trade. On shore leave between voyages he fell seriously ill, so ill that he realised that his ocean-going life was over. He secured employment in Liverpool as a Tide-waiter, a Customs Officer who boarded and inspected incoming ships. It was while living and working in Liverpool that he began to think seriously about religion. He was much influenced by evangelical preachers who came to Liverpool, men like George Whitfield.

This effect of this 'second instalment' of conversion led Newton to conclude that he was called to the ministry. But who would ordain a man with such a background? He offered himself for ordination but was refused by two Archbishops.

At this point he met Lord Dartmouth who was impressed by his sincerity and spoke on his behalf to the Bishop of Chester. The Bishop ordained Newton in 1764 and he could now accept the curacy at Olney offered him by Lord Dartmouth who was Patron of that Parish.

So began Newton's fifteen years as a country parson in Olney, first as Curate and later as Vicar. And it was there that his friendship began with the poet Cowper. In 1779 the two

William Cowper, poet and friend of John Newton.

St. Peter and St. Paul's, Olney.

friends, pastor and poet, published The Olney Hymns – the first such Hymnal ever to be published in England. Two hundred and eighty of the hymns were Newton's, and eighty were Cowper's. Of Newton's hymns undoubtedly the best known is 'Amazing Grace'. And how eloquently it expresses his extraordinary transformation from slave trader to Priest, and from profligacy to pastoral devotion.

'Amazing grace! How sweet the sound
that saved a wretch like me.
I once was lost but now I'm found,
was blind but now I see.

'Twas grace that taught my heart to fear,
and grace my fears relieved.
How precious did that grace appear
the hour I first believed.

Through many dangers, toils and snares
I have already come.
'Tis grace hath brought me safe thus far,
and grace will lead me home.

The Lord has promised good to me,
His word my hope secures.
He will my shield and portion be
as long as life endures.'

After fifteen years as country priest at Olney, Newton moved to London and became Vicar of St. Mary, Woolnoth. His ministry there lasted twenty-eight years. His move to London and his ministry there proved providential, for it brought him into contact with the MP, William Wilberforce, who for years had been battling to get the slave trade abolished. With his unique background as a former slave trader himself, Newton could give stalwart support to Wilberforce. Newton died at the age of eighty-two in 1807, the very year in which the shameful slave trade was at last abolished.

The Newton Window in Olney Church, honouring the former Slave Trader who became Vicar. (JH)

Newton was buried at St. Mary, Woolnoth and his tombstone was carved with an inscription of his own composition. Later his body was disinterred and moved to Olney Churchyard. His tombstone there still bears the inscription Newton had composed for himself:

JOHN NEWTON
Clerk
Once an infidel and libertine
A servant of Slaves in Africa
was
by the rich mercy of our Lord and Saviour

JESUS CHRIST

preserved, restored and pardoned
And appointed to Preach the Faith
he had long laboured to destroy

He ministered
near XVI years as Curate and Vicar
of Olney in Bucks and XXVIII as Rector of
these United Parishes

Truly, John Newton's place in the annals of country clerics must be as astonishing as any.

3. SCOTT OF OLNEY. 'THE COMMENTATOR.'

John Newton was succeeded at Olney by Thomas Scott, a priest with a prodigious reputation for his learning and his writings. He was born in 1747, the son of a sheep farmer in Lincolnshire. He served a curacy in Bucks at Weston Underwood before becoming Vicar of Olney. There, like John Newton, he became both friend and pastor to the poet Cowper.

Scott had already published his volume of Essays. Of this work, no less a person than Cardinal Newman later wrote:

'He made a deeper impression on my mind than any other,
and to him, humanly speaking, I almost owe my soul'.

In 1788 Scott began the great Commentary on the Bible which earned him the nickname of 'The Commentator'. For the next century Scott's Commentary commanded a huge readership. Sir James Stephen described it as 'the greatest theological performance of our age and country'.

After Olney, Scott went in 1801 to be Rector of Aston Sandford, and there in 1821 he died, aged seventy-four.

4. THE FORTUNE TELLER OF THORNTON.

Two small villages only a mile apart in north Bucks give us two country clerics with their own individual claims to fame.

In 1616 William Bredon became Rector of Thornton. He served the Parish for twenty-two years, dying in 1638. In the life of a small village parish it matters enormously that the Vicar should be both well-liked and a good pastor. If, in addition, he has some other attribute – perhaps some skill or interest or enthusiasm, then that will be a bonus. The village will be interested in their Rector's speciality. And that's how it was with the Reverend William Bredon. He was well-liked as a person and much appreciated for his pastoral care of the parish, and he had one special skill or interest – he could tell fortunes! His hobby and pre-occupation was astrology. He was very knowledgeable on the subject. In fact, he assisted Sir Christopher Heydon in writing his book, 'Judicial Astrology'. The Rector was able to predict anyone's future, provided he knew the zodiacal data obtaining at the time of his birth. So Bredon, some three hundred and fifty years ago, was offering the same service as is now offered in the 'What the Stars Foretell' columns of our newspapers today.

5. THE BOGUS VICAR OF THORNBOROUGH.

Just a mile away from Thornton there was and there is the village of Thornborough. To that village there came a new Rector in 1660. His name was Joseph Newell. He was made very welcome and soon showed himself an ideal country pastor. He served the parish faithfully for nearly thirty years. For all that time he was busy doing all the things that a good priest does – he taught the faith and administered the Sacraments. Year after year he celebrated the Holy Communion; he baptised, married and buried the members of his flock, *but he knew one thing which none of his parishioners knew.*

And that secret was the fact that the Reverend Joseph Newell wasn't a 'Reverend' at all ! He wasn't a Parson, and he never had been!

*Thornborough Church. For thirty years in the 17th century it had a bogus Rector.
(JH)*

How could that be? You may very well ask. And I cannot tell you. All I can do is to quote what Browne Willis wrote in his 'History of Buckingham' published in 1755. Browne Willis, writing a century or so after that strange episode in Thornborough, records the matter thus:

> *Joseph Newell, Anno Domini 1663. This person continued to serve this parish of Thornborough, though never in Orders, as I have been informed, for near thirty years. And though he took out the Bishop's Title, on November 7th 1688, being detected for Want of Orders, was obliged to retire and leave the Parish. He went to Pottersbury and died there I was told'.*

6. CORROSION AT DRAYTON BEAUCHAMP?

Isaac Walton is universally known as the author of 'The Compleat Angler'. But he also wrote biographies, one of which is of Bucks significance. It is the life of Richard Hooker. The Bucks connection is made clear by Walton. He wrote:

'By marriage this good man was drawn from the tranquility of his College: from that garden of piety, of pleasure, of peace, and a sweet conversation, into the thorny wilderness of a busy world; into those corroding cases that attend a married priest, and a country parsonage, which was Drayton Beauchamp in Buckinghamshire'.

Perhaps Walton was being less than fair to that village. In any case, in 1585 Hooker left his Bucks country living and went on to be Master of the Temple in London, and began work on his monumental 'Ecclesiastical Polity'. It is this great work, in eight volumes, to which Anglican theology owned its tone and direction for the succeeding centuries.

7. WILLIAM WOOLEY.
THE WITCH HUNTER OF WINGRAVE.

The alliteration makes this an irresistible but shameful headline.

William Wooley was Vicar of Wingrave from 1753 to 1783. In 1726 the draconian Statutes Against Witchcraft had been repealed. But surreptitiously the ill-treatment of suspected witches still continued, especially in rural areas.

So it came about in Wingrave Parish. Susanna Hannokes, an inoffensive old woman, was accused by one of her neighbours of bewitching her spinning wheel so that the owner could not make it go round. The owner of the spinning wheel and her husband 'took the case to Court' – in other words they laid a complaint on oath before a Magistrate. But they also 'took the case' to the Church. They demanded of the Vicar, the Revd. William Wooley, that the witch be subjected to trial by ordeal. And the Vicar agreed.

So Susanna was hauled to the church, stripped of her clothes even to her shift, and was weighed on a pair of scales against the Church Bible. Fortunately for Susanna, she outweighed the Bible and so was acquitted of the charge. Had she failed, she would next have been forced to undergo the ordeal of 'swimming'. Her hands and feet would have been tied together and she would have been dragged through the water. So that was one that William Wooley the Witch Finder did not win.

8. FROM PARSONAGE TO PALACE.

The CV of many a bishop or archbishop shows in its earliest entries a rural priestly origin. The Parish of Worminghall furnishes not one but two examples. John King was Bishop of London and was buried in St. Paul's Cathedral in 1621. But his ministry began in Worminghall.

His son, Henry King, also came from Worminghall. He went on to be Dean of Rochester and then, in 1641, Bishop of Chichester. He died in 1669.

In Whaddon Parish in 1500 Richard Cox was born. His early education was at nearby Snelshall Priory. He went on to be Bishop of Ely in 1559. He assisted in the preparation of the English Prayer Book of that year. He died in 1581.

In 1487 William Warham became Rector of the Church of St. James in Great Horwood. He never actually lived there, but appointed a curate to minister in his stead. He went on to become Chancellor of England and Archbishop of Canterbury. He it was who married Henry VIII and Catherine of Aragon. When that marriage was dissolved William Warham did his best to oppose the divorce and the marriage of Henry VIII to Anne Boleyn.

9. ATTERBURY – ELEVATED AND EXILED.

To the tiny village and parish of Milton Keynes (later to give its name to a great new town) a new Rector came in 1657. He lasted until 1693 when he was thrown from his horse while crossing the bridge at Newport Pagnell and was drowned. His name was Lewis Atterbury.

His son, Francis Atterbury, was born in the Milton Keynes Vicarage in 1662. He was destined to be far more famous than his father. He was educated at Westminster School. Later he held, in plurality, the offices of both the Bishop of Rochester and the Dean of Westminster.

His professional career was a stormy one. When James II abdicated and fled to France, making way for the crowning of William and Mary in 1688, all clergy were required to make the declaration of fidelity to the new monarchs. This Francis Atterbury refused to do. He was accused of plotting to try to bring back the Stuarts. He was deprived of all his offices and was briefly imprisoned in the Tower. On being released he was banished from the Kingdom in 1723. He spent the remainder of his life in exile in France. He died in 1732. His body was brought back to this country and was buried in an unmarked grave in Westminster Abbey.

10. GIBBS OF NEWPORT PAGNELL.

John Gibbs was vicar of Newport Pagnell in the 1650s, during the Protectorate of Oliver Cromwell. When the Monarchy was restored in 1660 Gibbs was ejected from the Vicarage. In the remaining years of his life (he died in 1669) he devoted himself to fostering independent congregations in and around Newport Pagnell.

The young John Gibbs had been educated at Bedford School. From there he went up to Sidney Sussex College, Cambridge. There he was required to study theology and was expected to proceed to ordination in the Church of England. He graduated in 1648 by which time he was a Congregationalist by conviction. In 1652 he was inducted to the Living of Newport Pagnell.

There is no evidence that he was ever ordained episcopally, or that he had received ordination through Presbyteriansim. In any case, throughout the 1650s he conducted a double ministration, simultaneously in the Parish Church and in the fostering of gathered congregations in and round Newport Pagnell.

When the monarchy was restored in 1660 the Convention Parliament passed an Act: 'For Comfirming and Restoring of Ministers'. The Act identified four categories:

First, ministers occupying Livings from which the legal incumbents had been ejected, must hand them back to the original ministers, if still alive.

Second, ministers who had secured Livings by keeping out legitimate applicants for those Livings, must make way for those they had displaced.

Third, ministers who had petitioned for the execution of Charles I, or had opposed the restoration of Charles II, must be ejected.

Fourth, ministers who had publicly denied the validity of infant baptism must be ejected.

It was on that fourth point that John Gibbs was ejected. He left the Vicarage and took up residence in the High Street, renting a small house behind which there was a barn. And in that barn the Newport Pagnell Gathered Church met for worship, with John Gibbs as their minister.

This was a risky business. Both the congregation and their minister were liable to arrest. They could be fined, or even imprisoned, for not worshipping in the Parish Church. Much later, in 1820, repairs were being made to the house which John Gibbs had rented. In the course of the work a hidden cupboard, four feet square, was discovered. The only way into it was by a trap door concealed in the chimney breast of the room below. This nonconformist's 'priest's hole' was found to contain some coat buttons, two small tobacco pipes and a few silver coins.

11. THE DEVIL IN THE BOOT.
John Schorne came from Monks Risborough to North Marston as Rector. He served the parish until his death in 1314. He earned a great reputation not only for his piety, but also for his skill in water divining, and for healing the sick. His fame spread far and wide. His tomb in North Marston Church became a shrine to which pilgrims flocked in great numbers. It was said that only Walsingham and Canterbury attracted more pilgrims.

Part of the legend built up around John Schorne was that he possessed the power to control the Devil by 'conjuring him into a boot'. Several inns adopted the 'Devil in the Boot' motif for their inn-signs.

The pilgrim traffic to North Marston brought the village and its church a considerable income. Schorne was never canonised as a saint, though many revered him as such.

Towards the end of the 15th century the King wanted a new St. George's Chapel to be built at Windsor. He had already appointed the Bishop of Salisbury as Dean of Windsor and he commissioned the Dean to create the new Chapel. The Dean decided that to raise the money needed for the project, he must

Pilgrims stayed here in North Marston until the Shrine was lost.

All that remains of John Schorne's Shrine in North Marston Church. (NK)

find a way of attracting pilgrims to Windsor. For that to happen, he needed a magnet – a holy shrine – to draw the pilgrims there. He thought that moving John Schorne's Shrine from North Marston to Windsor would serve the purpose very well. So he successfully applied to the Pope for permission to move John Schorne's bones to Windsor. Windsor's gain was North Marston's loss.

12. THE NOBLE ARMY OF MARTYRS.
TWO CENTURIES SEPARATE THE MARTYRDOMS
OF TWO CLERICS WITH BUCKS CONNECTIONS.

John Wycliff, 'the Morning Star of the Reformation', was presented to the living of Ludgershall. He exchanged his previous and richer living of Fillingham in Lincolnshire so that he might be nearer Oxford. Wycliff held the living of Ludgershall for eight years, until in 1376 he went to be Rector of Lutterworth.

During his tenancy at Ludgershall, although he spent most of his time in Oxford, he preached in the market towns of Bucks. Many of his followers (the Lollards) suffered martyrdom at Amersham and elsewhere. Wycliff was a powerful opponent of the claims of the Papcy. He also wrote a series of works attacking the wealth of the Church. He emphasised various points which were later central to the reformation. He argued that only Scripture offered a firm base for authority, and therefore the Scriptures must be available to all in their own language.

Wycliff. His followers were known as Lollards.

In 1381, by which time he was at Lutterworth, his opinions were declared heretical in Oxford and his trial was demanded. Before he could be tried he died at Lutterworth in 1384 and was buried there. But later his remains were dug up, burnt and flung in to the River Swift at Lutterworth.

* * *

In the churchyard of Chesham Church an Ionic Cross bears this inscription:

> *To the glory of God and to the memory of Thomas Harding,*
> *Martyr, of Dungrove, Chesham, who in fiery trial at the stake laid*
> *down his life for the Word of God and for the testimony of Jesus*
> *Christ in this parish on May 30th 1532.*
>> *'The Noble army of Martyrs praise Thee".'*

This is but one of the many persecutions featured in Foxe's Book of Martyrs. Harding, it is alleged, was condemned for 'speaking against idolatry and superstition'.

'Some to bear faggots, some were burned in the cheek with hot irons, some were condemned to perpetual prison, some thrust into monasteries, some compelled to make pilgrimages . . . to St. Romuld of Buckingham, some to the rood of Wendover, some to St. John Schorne' (see page 62).

13. TITHING.
POOR JOHN GOULD OF BEACONSFIELD.

You cannot study the rural ministry or the lives of country clerics without being made aware of the effect on their ministry in times past of the payment of Tithes.

A 'Tithe' is a 'tenth' and the idea of paying tithes was first mentioned in Scripture in the Book of Genesis. There we read of the vow which Jacob made: 'Of all that Thou shalt give me I will surely give the tenth to Thee'.

In the Early Middle Ages tithes were made a legal obligation on all landowners. Theoretically a tithe could be levied on every kind of product – field and root crops, hay, vegetables, timber, and even milk, honey, beeswax and the progeny of livestock!

In theory, the tithe should have been distributed in four parts: one for the Bishop, one for the maintenance of the fabric of the church, one for the Rector of the Parish, and one for the relief of the poor. In practice the greater part of the tithe, varying in amount from one parish to another, went to the Rector. It could be the source of endless bickering and resentment.

Peasants paying tithes.

The gradual abolition of Tithes began in England in 1836, and by 1868 the compulsory payment of Church Rates ceased. But until those changes came about, Tithes could be a persistent headache – resented by farmers and a constant anxiety to the clergy.

Let us consider the experience of the Reverend John Gould, Rector of St. Mary and All Saints in Beaconsfield. He had a very chequered career as a country cleric. He was Rector of his parish for forty-six years and when he died in 1866 he was a prisoner in Newgate for debt.

Poor John Gould, for most of his ministry he had a running

The Boundary Stone at Beaconsfield.

quarrel with his local farmers over matters of tithes. This was not unique to Beaconsfield – it applied in countless places. Friction between the clergy and the farmers was reflected in the well-known jingle:

'We've cheated the Parson, we'll cheat him again
For why should the Vicar have one in ten?'

In Beaconsfield the farmers were particularly resistant to the payment of tithes and they had their own ways of tackling the problem. They claimed that if the tithe on their corn was taken *after* it had been stacked into shocks for drying, they should be credited for the extra labour involved. They computed the cost as entitling them to paying only one every *eleven* shocks, not one in ten. The Vicar disputed this. The farmers erected a Tithing Stone at Holtspor near Beaconsfield. It is dated 1827 and it is still there. Its inscription reads:

'The custom of tithing corn in this parish is (and has been so
immemmoriably) by the tenth Cock and the eleventh Shock'.

Poor John Gould indeed. He lost the Battle of the Tithes, and he lost his life, dying in a debtor's prison in 1866.

14. SPORTING PARSONS.

One such was the Rector of Simpson, always known as Tally Ho! Hanmer. He was addicted to hunting and dressed accordingly. He sported mahogany-coloured top boots, a square-cut riding coat, with black breeches, crowned by a peculiar black hat with a broad flat brim.

He was constantly in debt and spent quite a time in a Debtor's Prison. He sponged shamelessly on his friends and neighbours and he loved to go up to London to dine and to attend the theatre.

Yet for all that, he was popular in his parish, charitable to the poor and could preach excellent sermons. J. K. Fowler wrote of him:

'His rectory was generally barricaded against creditors throughout
the week. Only on Sundays could he walk about in its grounds
and visit his parishioners. Tally Ho! Hanmer was a rollicking
jolly sportsman, a bachelor, of a type of class once very prevalent in
England. For good or ill such men are no more.'

* * *

It is almost refreshing to leave such examples of 'clerical error' in earlier centuries and to turn instead to the story of the great sporting parson of Passenham. He was not only the Vicar of Passenham, he was also a Magistrate. And he was a sportsman with a great liking for prize fighting. In fact he was himself a great pugilist. He was the Reverend Loraine Smith and he lived about a hundred and fifty years ago.

Prize fighting was illegal. Despite this Loraine Smith himself helped to arrange some prize fights. Passenham being so close to the Bucks./Northants. border, it was easy to switch at the last minute from one side of the border to the other to avoid police harassment. But the conflict between his sporting instincts and his conscience as a Magistrate posed problems for the sporting parson. On one occasion he had been obliged, as a Magistrate, to help the police organise a raid on an illegal prize fight. The police managed to stop the fight and the crowd scattered. But when the police tried to arrest one of the fighters he simply laid out the constables! It was then left to the Magistrate/Parson/Pugilist Loraine Smith to arrest the offender. But he let him go again with no more than a friendly caution.

* * *

The great 18th century clerical wit, the Reverend Sydney Smith, once said, 'What a pity it is that we have no amusements in England but vice and religion'. It could be said, perhaps, that clerical errors often neatly combine the two.

Chapter Four

TWO LITERARY GIANTS
BUNYAN OF BEDFORD
AND MILTON IN BUCKS

Both were puritans. Both were Roundhead in sympathy. They shared the 17th century. Each addressed religion in his own way. And both have achieved universal fame.

1. JOHN BUNYAN. 'CHIEF OF SINNERS.'

The world knows him as the author of 'The Pilgrim's Progress', but he wrote more than fifty other books or tracts. And he wrote his own autobiography, calling it 'Grace Abounding to the Chief of Sinners'.

John Bunyan was born in 1628 and died in 1688. He was born at Elstow near Bedford and went to school there. His favourite reading was Ballads and Chapbook versions of chivalrous romances. His father was a tinker or brasier and John expected to follow his father in the same trade. But at the age of sixteen he was enrolled in the Parliamentary army to serve in the Civil War. His service lasted from 1644 to 1647 and kept him at Newport Pagnell where his regiment was garrisoned. Not much is known about his time in Cromwell's army, except that he himself recorded a providential escape from death. A fellow soldier had taken John's place at a siege and was killed.

The young Bunyan was much influenced by the Puritans by whom he was surrounded and by the preachers who served them. In 1647, discharged from the Army, he began work as a travelling tinker. He married in 1648 at the age of twenty, and ran into a psychological crisis. His young wife owned two books which John read. They were: Arthur Dent's 'The Plain Man's Pathway to

John Bunyan

St. John's, Bedford. Bunyan was baptised here.

The cottage in which John Bunyan was born in Elstow.

Heaven', and Lewis Bayley's 'The Practice of Piety'. Their effect on him was profound. They convinced him that he was a sinner destined for Hell! He decided that he must reform, change his whole way of life and strive for salvation. Out went dancing and bell-ringing which he loved, and in came intense study of scripture. In his search for spiritual enlightenment, he found help and solace in contact with members of such religious sects as Ranters and Quakers. He read some of their books but did not always agree with them. In his study of Scripture he was very influenced by Luther's Commentary on Galatians, and later wrote that in it he found his own spiritual condition so exactly mirrored that it was as if Luther's book had been 'written out of my heart'.

In 1653 he joined an Independent or Congregationalist Church in Bedford but he had not yet won through to a settled conviction, but rather was alternating between moods of black despair and occasional visions of ecstasy. Three years later be began preaching. This brought him into conflict with the establishment, for authority considered it wrong that 'unlearned and unordained men,' should preach. So Bunyan, like other 'mechanick preachers' was attacked by the regular clergy. But sometimes also Bunyan found himself at odds with some of the other independent preachers and he began to attack them in writing as well as verbally. He wrote Tracts which in turn brought Tracts in rebuttal from those he criticised. Gaining in experience, Bunyan produced more considered theological writing. In 1659 he published 'The Doctrine of Law and Grace Unfolded', a book developing the twin covenants of Calvinist theology – works and grace.

His first wife died and he married a second wife a year later in 1659. In 1660 the restoration of the monarchy under Charles II brought an end to the freedom that Puritans had enjoyed under Cromwell. From this point onwards nonconformist preachers like Bunyan found themselves increasingly harried. In November 1660 Bunyan was arrested at Lower Samsell. The Magistrate remanded him in custody to appear before the Quarter Sessions in Bedford in January 1661. So began a series of imprisonments which were to last for twelve years.

*John
Bunyan's
Arrest
Warrant.*

He used his time in gaol to make shoe laces for sale to support his family, and in preaching to his fellow inmates. And, of course, he continued his writing. His first prison book was 'Profitable Meditations' (1661). Next year came 'I Will Pray with the Spirit', and a year later, 'Christian Behaviour'. And, more importantly, he made a start on 'The Pilgrim's Progress'.

In 1672 Charles II made a Declaration of Indulgence, granting a Royal Pardon to imprisoned unlawful preachers. So Bunyan was not only released, but was also given a licence to preach. He wasted no time and was soon preaching constantly – in Bedfordshire, Cambridgeshire and Hertfordshire. The wags gave him the nickname of 'Bishop Bunyan', which he probably didn't appreciate!

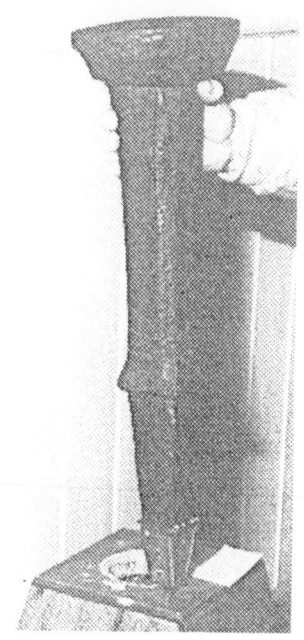

*Door of John Bunyan's prison
in Silver Street.*

Bunyan's Anvil.

A second spell of imprisonment came in 1677, this time lasting six months. It was during this time that he completed his great masterpiece, 'The Pilgrim's Progress'. It was an instant success. By the time Bunyan died in 1688 a dozen or more authorised editions had been published. The book was also published in New England. Translations also appeared – in French, Dutch and Welsh.

His other writings continued too. He published 'The Life and Death of Mr Badman' in 1680, 'The Holy War in 1682. And in 1684, because a spurious continuation of 'The Pilgrim's Progress' had appeared, he published his own official Second Part of the great classic.

His death, in August 1688, was brought about by a fever contracted while riding back from London in heavy rain. He was buried in the famous Dissenting Burial Ground at Bunhill Fields, Finsbury.

His work as a travelling tinker made him very familiar with the countryside of his native Bedfordshire. Readers of 'The Pilgrim's Progress' have enjoyed identifying places and features in the book with actual Bed's geography. Thus, when he wrote of 'The River of the Water of Life', this was The Great Ouse, in its summer mood, with Christian and his companion walking happily in the riverside meadows. But the sombre river in its winter mood is also there. Then it becomes 'The River of Death' which must be crossed even though there is no bridge. That river was deep and dangerous, but Christian was told: 'You must go through, or you cannot come at the Gate'. His 'Hill Difficulty' was probably the hill at Ampthill, and his 'House Beautiful' was inspired by Houghton House. And no doubt for Bunyan 'the Delectable Mountains' were The North Chilterns.

2. JOHN MILTON.
'GOD-GIVEN ORGAN-VOICE OF ENGLAND.'

It was Tennyson who wrote that about Milton, the greatest epic poet in the English language. Buckinghamshire cannot claim him as a native-born son, but he lived for a while in this county, and he completed 'Paradise Lost', and began work on 'Paradise Regained', at Chalfont St. Giles.

He was born in Bread Street in 1608 in Cheapside, the son of a composer of some distinction. He attended St. Paul's School and went up to Christ's College, Cambridge, where he spent seven years. He died in 1674 and was buried next to his father in Cripplegate.

For five years, 1632 to 1637, he lived with his parents at Horton in Northants and his mother is buried there. While at Horton he wrote; *Lycidas, Il Pensero, L'Allegro,* and the *Masque Comus* which he wrote for production at Ludlow Castle.

His period of residence in Bucks was brief but dramatic. It lasted only about a year. It was Chalfont St. Giles to which Milton came in 1665, fleeing from the plague in London. By then he was blind. But despite this handicap it was at Chalfont St. Giles that he completed his masterpiece, 'Paradise Lost', and began work on 'Paradise Regained'.

John Milton c. 1629. (Artist unknown.)

His house at Chalfont St. Giles is now the Milton Museum. In 1887 the house was almost lost. It was planned to demolish it brick by brick and to transport it for re-erection in America. Happily, the plan was scotched. A Public Subscription was raised to save the building. Queen Victoria personally donated £20, and Queen Elizabeth II visited the Museum in 1987 to celebrate the Centenary of the Appeal.

Quite apart from his poetic genius, Milton's life was quite

astonishing in the range of his activities. He was, at different times, a would-be ordinand, a classical scholar, a traveller, a teacher, a polemicist and pamphleteer, and a Civil Servant. His matrimonial history was somewhat turbulent and he married three times. Divorce was the subject of four of his pamphlets.

In religion he became a Puritan and in the Civil War he was an ardent anti-royalist and Parliamentarian. It followed therefore that at the Restoration of the monarchy in 1660 he was *persona non grata* and he feared imprisonment. In fact however he was left unmolested.

John Milton's life falls into three distinct phases. (So do his marriages!) The first phase saw Milton as the brilliant Cambridge scholar. His first poems were written at Cambridge. After Cambridge came visits to Italy and then he settled down with his parents at Horton. He regarded this period as the real preparation for his life's work as a poet. Earlier, while still at Cambridge, he had wondered whether he was destined for the ministry. That possibility dropped from his mind in the Horton period and all his concentration there was on the making of poetry – in Latin and Italian as well as in English. His studies included Greek as well as Latin, and he devoted time also to a study of the Church Fathers. For two years also he undertook the tutoring of his nephews.

The second phase of his life lasted from 1640 to 1660. Significantly this period covers the whole of the Civil War and of the Commonwealth under Cromwell. Throughout that time he wrote virtually no poetry at all. Instead, he was caught up in the great issues of the day – the struggle between King and Parliament, the issues of liberty and authority, and Puritanism. He became at once both a polemicist and a pamphleteer. His writings attacked episcopacy, advanced fierce arguments against censorship, and advocated the right to terminate marriage by divorce.

In 1649 he became Latin Secretary to Cromwell's Council. Foreign correspondence at that time was still conducted in Latin as being the only truly international language. After the King's execution, an event which shocked the countries of Europe, Milton as Latin Secretary became the chief apologist for the

Commonwealth. He wrote a number of papers defending the execution and the regicides who had signed the Death Warrant.

His duties to the Council perforce ceased when the Monarchy was restored. For a while he went into hiding, fearing arrest and punishment for the prominent role he had played under Cromwell. But his fears were relieved by the passing of the Act of Indemnity and Oblivion. So, now no longer a quasi-Civil Servant, he resumed his life and work as a poet. The third and last phase of his remarkable career had begun.

But before we turn to that last so fruitful phase, which was to give the world 'Paradise Lost', 'Paradise Regained', and 'Samson Agonistes', we have to take note of the fact that from 1652 onwards his eyesight had deteriorated until he was finally blind. And besides this physical handicap there were also personal tragedies.

In 1642, at the age of thirty-four, Milton had married a girl half his age. The young wife soon left him and this is what had prompted the writing of those four pamphlets advocating divorce. But later the young wife returned and three daughters were born, before she died in 1652.

The widower's blindness drew from him a stoical sonnet, 'On his blindness'. The opening line is: 'When I consider how my light is spent', and the final line of the sonnet is still more familiar; 'They also serve who only stand and wait'.

In his final years his daughters, now young adults, became his eyes. They took turns in reading to him and sharing in the work of writing down the blank verse which issued in increasing volume from his poetic muse.

In 1656 Milton married for the second time. But Katherine died only two years later, after giving birth to a daughter who survived only a few months. In 1663 he married a third time – Elizabeth Minshull. To escape the plague in London they fled to Chalfont St. Giles and there 'Paradise Lost' was completed.

It was Milton's friend, Thomas Ellwood, who arranged for the Miltons to settle in the cottage at Chalfont St. Giles. And it is Ellwood who is reputed to have said to John Milton, 'Thou hast said much here of 'Paradise Lost', but what hast thou to say of paradise found?' So Milton was moved to begin work at Chalfont on 'Paradise Regained'. It was published, along with 'Samson Agonistes', when Milton returned to London in 1671. Three years later, in 1674, John Milton died.

Three other poets have paid their testimony to Milton's genius. Tennyson wrote of him:

'God-given organ-voice of England,
Milton, a name to resound for ages'.

Byron wrote of:

'Milton, the Prince of Poets'.

And Cowper, that quintessentially Buckinghamshire poet, once wrote:

'Greece, sound thy Homer's, Rome, thy Virgil's name,
But England's Milton equals both in fame'.

Chapter Five

JOURNEY FOR A DEAD QUEEN, LINCOLN TO WESTMINSTER

The journey began in Lincoln on 4th December 1290, and ended in Westminster on 17th December 1290. But metaphorically, it began long before that, and in a place far remote from Lincoln. The story really began at Burgos in Northern Spain in 1254. In that year and at that place a ten year old princess, Eleanor, daughter of King Ferdinand of Castille, was betrothed to an English prince, Edward, the future King Edward I of England. In due time the young prince married the princess, and their marriage lasted thirty-six years. Queen Eleanor bore King Edward I fifteen children – four boys and eleven girls.

In the early winter of 1290 the Royal Household was on the move, making a Royal Progress towards Scotland. In late November the Queen fell ill of a low fever. She was taken to the Manor House at Harby, six miles west of Lincoln. There, on 28th November 1290, she died. The King was grief-stricken. He said, 'I loved her dearly during her life time, and I shall not cease to love her now that she dead'. He resolved that Queen Eleanor's body should be carried to Westminster and that, at each place where her body rested, a cross should be erected.

First, her body was taken to Lincoln and there it was embalmed. Her entrails were buried in Lincoln Cathedral, and the first of the Eleanor Crosses were erected at the foot of Cliff Hill in Lincoln.

From Lincoln to Grantham, twenty-three miles, was the longest day's passage of the Funeral Procession. There, the second Cross was erected. And so on, another twenty miles to Stamford, where the body rested again and a third Cross was erected in Scotgate.

A further seventeen miles and the journey had extended to Geddington, where the fourth Eleanor Cross still stands, outside the Church of St. Mary, Magdalene, in which the Queen's body rested overnight.

Next, crossing on the bridge over the River Ise, Eleanor's funeral journey continued another nineteen miles to Northampton, reaching there on 9th December 1290. Her body lay for the night in Delapré Abbey at Hardinstone. There today the modern traffic of a busy road still passes within yards of Eleanor's Cross, two miles out of Northampton.

Left: *The original Eleanor Cross at Charing Cross, since replaced.*
Right: *The Eleanor Cross at Geddington.*

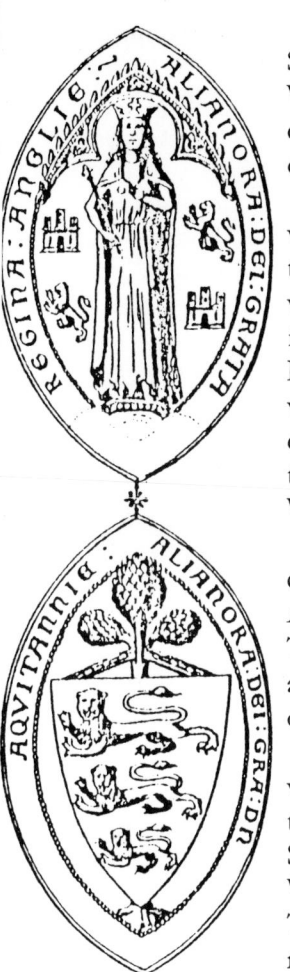

Queen Eleanor's Seals.

A shorter run then, only twelve miles to Stony Stratford, crossing the River Ouse by Watling Street. The Cross here has long since disappeared, and modern buildings now stand on its former site in High Street.

Another eleven miles, and so to Woburn, where the Abbey was in temporary decline at the time. Woburn's Eleanor Cross, now gone, was erected in the Market Place. A short run further brought the Royal Funeral Procession to Dunstable Priory. The Prior sprinkled with holy water the place where the Cross should be erected, at the point in the Market Place where the ancient Icknield way met the equally ancient Watling Street.

By the evening of the 13th December the dead Queen's body could rest in St. Albans Abbey, and an all-night vigil was kept there. Today the Clock Tower in the High Street bears a plaque recording the fact that Eleanor's Cross once stood there.

King Edward had so far accompanied his wife's body but, after Dunstable, he went ahead to await her in London. Meanwhile, from St. Albans, Eleanor's body was taken to Waltham and there rested in Waltham Abbey. The tenth Eleanor Cross, more elaborate than most, marked the passage of the dead Queen.

As the procession travelled on from Waltham Cross towards London, the King, accompanied by all the nobility and the prelates, came out to meet it. Within the capital, in due time, the eleventh and twelfth Crosses were erected at West Cheap and at Charing. The exact site of the Charing Cross was at the junction of Whitehall and Trafalgar Square. It was this Cross which was later replaced by the Cross which stands today some two hundred yards to the east in the forecourt of Charing Cross Station, created by

Victorian mason Thomas Earp, who used 13th century Gothic motifs, repeated in the Albert Memorial.

So ended the unique journey of the dead Queen Eleanor. She reached her final resting place in Westminster Abbey on the 17th December 1290. Her tomb is regarded as one of the finest examples of medieval craftsmanship. Richard Crundale, the Master Mason of Charing Cross, made her tomb, and another craftsman, Thomas of Leighton Buzzard was responsible for its fine iron grille.

For a month after his wife's interment King Edward stayed in retreat at Ashridge. A contemporary account of his melancholia after this bereavement was written by the monk, Piers of Langtoft:

'His solace all was reft sith she was from him gone.
On fell things he thought, and waxed as heavy as lead,
For sadness him o'ermastered since Eleanor was dead'.

Sadly, of the twelve Eleanor Crosses erected in the 13th century, eight were destroyed by Parliamentary forces in the Civil War in the 17th century.

Chapter Six

FROM MONASTERIES TO MANSIONS IN BUCKS

The steady evolution over the centuries which has given us our manor houses, mansions, and stately homes has from time to time been dramatically interrupted. The Black Death in 1348 carried off a third of the population, leading to an appalling shortage of labour. It led of necessity to a great change in agriculture, marked by a wholesale switch to the rearing of sheep. And that in turn required the enclosure of lands which formerly had been open fields. All these things greatly affected the Manors.

In the 15th century came the Wars of the Roses, and in the 17th century the Civil War. Both conflicts profoundly affected landowners and Lords of the Manors. They had to decide whom to support – White Rose or Red in the first, and King or Parliament in the second. For many the wrong choice was catastrophic.

DISSOLUTION

We now consider a different kind of upheaval, the Reformation in the 16th century. In four short years, 1536 to 1540, many thousands of monastic houses were suppressed. Their property was transferred to the Crown as a means of increasing royal revenue.

There had been earlier signs that such a sensational crisis was looming. Henry III had received a pamphlet, written by a certain Simon Fish. The pamphlet accused the religious houses of being full of 'idle beggars and vagabonds who have gotten into their hands more than a third part of all your Realm'. Simon Fish went on to claim that the Monasteries and Priories have 'the goodliest Lordships, Manors, lands and territories'.

Though the population at large would not have agreed with such forthright anticlericalism, there was a growing body of opinion that perhaps the immense wealth of the monks and friars should be transferred to more deserving hands. Some of the clergy themselves shared the reforming spirit of the age and said that monastic wealth might well be appropriated and devoted to the endowment of charitable, educational and social enterprises.

Henry VIII looked to the Dissolution of the monasteries to give him huge and instant relief in his own needs for royal revenue. Parliament could see in the Dissolution a way of easing the pressure of increased taxation. Landowners saw the possibility of enlarging their estates. Merchants and the urban middle class thought that through the Dissolution they too might join the landed gentry.

Cardinal Wolsey had anticipated by a few years the main Dissolution. He ordered the closing of a number of smaller abbeys and priories. He wanted their revenues to enable him to carry out his own educational plans. The Priories at Wing and Ravenstone, and Bradwell Abbey, were among those closed as part of this programme. This enabled Wolsey to proceed with the foundation of Cardinal College in Oxford, which afterwards became Christ Church.

Another Priory which fell victim to Wolsey's search for revenue for his new college was Tickford Priory near Newport Pagnell. But it is hard to sympathise with Tickford. Its Priory for a long time had an unenviable reputation for scandal. Fulk Paganell had founded Tickford in 1140. It was a French-based order and for a while it did well. But during the Hundred Years War with France it was declared an 'alien' priory and its income was seized by the king. It was not at that point closed down, but neither did its reputation improve. It was more than once castigated by the Bishop of Lincoln for the laxity of its monks. In 1340 the monks indulged in virtual warfare with the Priest and Parish of Newport Pagnell, and Tickford's reputation did not mend thereafter. So in 1524 Wolsey was happy to close down what he called 'the superfluous House of Tickford' and to divert its revenue to his new Oxford College.

Another 'alien' Priory to suffer because of its French origin and connections was the Newton Longville Priory which had been founded by Walter Giffard, Lord of Longueville in Normandy. It was closed down in 1414. In 1441 its lands were seized by Henry VI and their revenue granted to New College, Oxford.

Some of the finance which flowed from the main Dissolution was spent for the nation's good – on the fortification of harbours and the development of arsenals, for example. And the king himself founded Trinity College in Cambridge in 1546. But these were exceptions. In the main it was the king himself who principally benefitted. But so too did the families to whom was passed the lands and tithes and, in many cases, the monastic buildings themselves of the suppressed religious houses.

The Dissolution was a two-stage operation. First came the closing of three hundred and seventy four religious houses with an income below a certain level. That happened in 1536. Then, between 1538 and 1540 what were described as 'great and solemn monasteries' were closed. They numbered one hundred and eighty six. And that made the Dissolution total. There were no exceptions – literally every last monastery, priory and nunnery was closed. A Court of Augmentation was set up to process the assets thus released.

Asa Briggs, in his 'Social History of England', says that some of the seized land was given away, subject to feudal knight service to be rendered by the recipients to the king. Other lands were sold, the price being fixed at a minimum of twenty times the annual rent.

It is said that two out of every three peers were either granted, or were allowed to purchase, monastic estates. The effect was that the lands tended to go into the hands of existing landowners, the peerage and the gentry. Only a relatively small proportion of it went to speculators. Asa Briggs goes on to describe how the naves of abbey churches in some cases became farmhouses, chantries became parlours, and towers became kitchens. Here a priory became a factory, there a furnace and forge were set up, and in a third place priory buildings were turned into a theatre.

When the young Edward VI came to the throne following the death of his father, Henry VIII in 1547, a further dissolution of religious properties was effected. These were the Guilds and Chantry Chapels. As such they were not monastic foundations, and their closure was simply a sort of corollory to the main wholesale dissolution which had already been completed.

While some of the proceeds from this second kind of dissolution undoubtedly went to found grammar schools, hospitals and almshouses, in many other cases speculators lined their own pockets. A good example of this is furnished by Fenny Stratford. There, back in 1494, the Guild of St. Catherine and St. Margaret had been founded. It used for worship a Chantry Chapel which had been built half a century before. In 1547 when all Guilds were abolished, the Fenny Chantry Chapel was pulled down, having been sold to three London speculators – 'certain sons of Belial' as someone described them. They carried off the building materials for sale or use elsewhere.

In the case of Bradwell Abbey, suppressed by Wolsey, the Cardinal sent a surveyor to appraise the buildings with a view to their sale. Purchasers were found for the various buildings. Some of the Priory buildings became barns, and the Prior's lodging became a farmhouse. What happened subsequently is interesting. A new Manor House was built by the Longville family on the site of the former Abbey. The Longvilles continued in occupation from 1543 until 1650. During the Civil War Thomas Longville was taken prisoner at Grafton in 1643. He survived the ordeal and was able to repossess his Manor in 1646 on payment of a fine of £800. That same year he was knighted by Charles I.

In 1650 Sir Thomas Longville sold the Manor to Sir John Lawrence who in his turn sold it to Sir Joseph Alston of Chelsea. Sir Joseph was created a Baron and took as his title Baron of Chelsea and Bradwell Abbey. The Alston family occupied the Manor, enlarging and improving it, until 1716.

But it was all downhill after that. By the 19th century the Manor was reduced to no more than a farmhouse. In the 20th century, improbably, it passed into the ownership of the Wolverton Co-op Society! In 1971 The Milton Keynes Development Corporation bought it and made it the Headquarters for its Archaeological staff. It thus became, and remains, the Bradwell Abbey Field Centre.

In common with all other counties, Bucks had a certain number of monastic foundations, though they were fewer and smaller than elsewhere. Reed, in his 'History of Buckinghamshire', has a map of the county showing the number and location of Bucks religious houses. There were twenty-four of them, and they are evenly spread, from Lavendon in the north to Medmenham and Burnham in the south.

In 1565 John Fortescue, a kinsman of Elizabeth I, held high office at Court and became a very wealthy man. He acquired the ancient Manor of Salden, near Mursley. He set to work to build a great manson there, palatial in its size, and worthy of his status as he saw it. His appetite for more land was whetted and he bought the three adjoining Manors of Shenley, Winslow and Drayton Parslow. But still he wanted more, so he acquired the land belonging to the suppressed Snelshall Priory. Unfortunately, though, Fortescue lost virtually everything he had, for being on the losing side in the Civil War. The Fortescue family fortune sank below solvency level and much of the land had to be sold off. When the Fortescue title became extinct in 1729 the great and palatial Salden Manor could not survive. By 1743 it had been totally demolished.

WOBURN

The most notable of all the monastic abbeys to be suppressed in this area, and the clearest example of a dissolution leading directly to the creation of a great mansion and stately home, is Woburn. Woburn Abbey was a Cistercian foundation. Hugh de Colebec founded it in 1145. It soon flourished and acquired many estates, including Swanbourne, Shenley, Wavendon, Bow Brickhill and Woughton. An offshoot or cell of Woburn Abbey was set up as far away as Medmenham on the banks of the Thames near Henley. This distant 'satellite' of Woburn Abbey was subsequently annexed to Bisham Abbey. After the Dissolution, the Medmenham Priory had its own astonishing 'after life' in the shape of the peculiar activities of Sir Francis Dashwood. But that is another story. *(See Chapter Sixteen.)*

At Woburn Abbey itself the dissolution in 1540 was marked by the execution, no less, of its last Prior or Abbot. He was Robert Hobs and he was hanged from an oak tree outside the Abbey's main gate. He had evidently been unwilling to go quietly and publicly challenged the King's claim to supremacy in Church affairs.

As well as being the largest of the religious houses to be suppressed in this part of the country, Woburn was also the wealthiest. Its gross income was ten times greater than any other local priory. On Dissolution its estates all went to the King, who immediately bestowed them on John Russell, Baron of Chenies, the ancestor of the Dukes of Bedford.

It was the 4th Duke of Bedford who rebuilt Woburn in its present form in the 18th century. He employed Thomas Moore to carry out the work. The quadrangular pattern of the old monastic buildings was retained, and though all is new above ground, the original crypt remains and today houses some of the many treasures of the great stately home.

CHICHELEY

Another great stately home is Chicheley. In the Middle Ages it too was monastic property. At the Dissolution it was sold to Anthony Cave, a rich London merchant. He built a new house there. The property passed to the Chester family. Anthony Chester, who became a baronet in 1620, fought on the Royalist side in the Civil War and commanded cavalry at the Battle of Naseby. Following that battle Chicheley was attacked and sacked. With the restoration of the monarchy under Charles II the family fortune revived and Sir John Chester built the present Chicheley Hall between 1698 and 1703. In 1952 Chicheley was bought by David, 2nd Earl Beatty.

HUGHENDEN

Hughenden Manor had a checkered history. It was one of the many manors awarded to Odo, Bishop of Bayeux at the Conquest. With all the rest it was taken away from him when he supported Robert's abortive attempt to succeed his father, William I. Henry I bestowed Hughenden on his Chancellor, Geoffrey de Clinton, who gave the Manor to the Priory of Kenilworth which he had founded in 1122. Hughenden remained monastic until the Dissolution of Monasteries in 1538. It was then awarded to Sir Robert Dormer who also owned the Manors of West Wycombe and Wing. By 1737 Hughenden had come into the possession of the Dormer-Stanhope family. The head of the family was the 4th Earl of Chesterfield. He disposed of it to the brothers Savage. In 1848 a new owner acquired it – he was Benjamin Disraeli, no less.

* * *

We should also note, briefly, other Bucks houses which have monastic connections in their past history.

Aston Abbots figured in Domesday as Estones. It became the property of St. Albans Abbey for several centuries.

Lavendon was an Abbey founded by John de Bedun in the reign of Henry II. It lasted until the Dissolution. In 1625 a farm, The Grange, was built on its site.

Biddlesden Park, on the Bucks/Northants border, was once a Cistercian Abbey.

Hillesden once belonged to the Monks of Notley Abbey, and it is they who built Hillesden Church.

Soulbury, for many centuries the seat of the Lovett family, once had a Chantry founded by Robert Lovett in 1301.

Chapter Seven

LOST PROPERTY
IN GREATER MILTON KEYNES

In the days before banks, safes and safety-deposit boxes, if you owned something and wanted to be sure to keep it, you hid it. And if you stole something, and wanted to be sure you could keep it, you hid it. And if there was something of value for which you were responsible but which was under threat, you hid it.

In all these cases it mattered a great deal *where* you hid it, and *how*. Nobody must see you put it there, and nobody watch you retrieve it. All of which is by way of introduction to the recounting of just a few of the finds that have been made in the greater Milton Keynes area from time to time.

A quite special kind of discovery was made in Granborough last century. Restoration work was being carried out in the nave of the Church. Embedded in the wall there was found a small leaden casket, measuring 6x2x2 inches. Inside the casket were three round receptacles. It was a Chrismatory – that is, a set of three containers for Holy Oil used in the Catholic Church for annointing at Baptism and Confirmation, and for Extreme Unction. There can be little doubt that the Chrismatory was hidden at the time of the Reformation, when the English Prayer Book replaced the Latin Missal and changes were ordered in the manner of administering Sacraments. One can imagine that such changes were not welcomed by the Parish Priest at that time and that he decided to hide the Holy Oil casket.

There was another discovery made in Granborough too. It was of a small alabaster panel of the Crucifixion, with the figures of St. John and the Virgin Mary on either side of the cross. It was found, improbably, built into the gable of a house in the village. No doubt it too had originally been in the Church and was removed and hidden at the time of the Reformation. It is now safely back in the Church.

In the little village of Broughton, which is a rural enclave just within the Milton Keynes boundary, stands the 14th century church of St. Lawrence. The Church is technically redundant and is now vested in, and the responsiblity of the Redundant Churches Fund. Though redundant, the church is still used for occasional services. It is a listed building, its architectural and artistic importance recognised.

What makes it particularly important is that the walls are covered by a unique set of medieval mural paintings. These paintings were for a long time 'lost' and needed to be re-discovered. They were lost (and forgotten) because at some time in the distant past the walls were whitewashed. In 1849 parts of them were accidentally uncovered. Since then they have all been uncovered and remain so, and are now being restored.

They are acknowledged to be of tremendous importance. They depict the Last Judgement, the Deposition (what the Creed refers

St. Helen, mother of the first Christian Emperor, in Broughton Church's fine medieval murals. (NK)

to as the descent of Jesus into Hades at His death and before His resurrection), St. George, St. Eligius, and St. Helena. St. George is the patron saint of England; St. Eligius, who was also known as St. Eloi, was born in 588 and died in 659 in Flanders. He was Bishop of Noyon and was regarded by many as the Patron Saint of goldsmiths and metalworkers; St. Helena was the mother of Constantine, the first Christian Emperor. She was credited with having found part of the cross on which Christ was crucified.

St. Andrew's Church at Great Linford is the scene of two other discoveries. The first happened after a partial collapse of part of the structure in 1865. This necessitated repairs, in the course of which entry had to be made into a vault below. The vault was, and is, the burial place of the Pritchard family. Sir William Pritchard died in 1704, and was buried there. His wife and son, who died later, were also buried there. These facts are commemorated in the Church itself on a large white marble monument. When the vault had to be entered, no-one was surprised to find the coffins there. But what did occasion surprise was the discovery that the son's coffin was standing upright at the foot of Sir William's coffin. The explanation is said to be that the son so idolised his father that he had let it be known that when he died he wanted to be buried at his father's feet, as it were continually paying homage.

The other discovery at St. Andrew's was made in 1980. In that year a service trench had to be dug across the north side of the churchyard. This uncovered a number of medieval burial sites. It was in one of these that a dramatic discovery was made – the skeletal remains of a young man. Expert examination of the bones showed that the deceased had died in his early twenties and had been of slight build. But what dramatically heightened interest in this particular burial was the presence in his grave of a chalice and paten. They were of a style and design of the 13th century. In medieval times it was the invariable practice, when a priest died, to bury with him his communion vessels. Usually, and for obvious reasons, these would be base metal copies rather than originals of precious metals. The ones found at Great Linford were of pewter.

13th century pewter chalice and paten found in a priest's grave in Great Linford's hurchyard. Who was he?

Who this priest was is not known. He cannot be identified with any of the clergy listed in the south aisle as Rectors of Great Linford. The fact that he appears to have died in his early twenties in any case would make it unlikely that he was ever the Parish Priest. It is also surprising that he was buried in the churchyard rather than in the chancel. All in all it seems likely that he was just a visitor to Great Linford, had fairly recently been ordained and had died during his visit.

Chapter Eight

LENGTH OF YEARS, MOULSOE

Nicholas Bloddington was presented to the Parish of Moulsoe as Rector in 1223 by the Prioress of Goring. David Morgan-Evans was presented to the Parish of Moulsoe as Rector in 1938 by Lord Carrington, father of the former Foreign Secretary. He retired in 1985 but Lord Carrington said that he could continue to live at the Rectory.

His official tenure as Rector, therefore, was forty-seven years, from 1938 to 1985. In his last years as Rector he had the distinction of being the oldest serving clergyman in the Church of England.

You might suppose that in the long line of Rectors of Moulsoe, from Nicholas Bloddington to Morgan-Evans, that the latter's tenure would be the longest. Not so. His '47 not out' is handsomely exceeded by Richard Cautley, who put in no less than fifty-six years as Rector before dying on 28th February 1842. Cautley's widow, Octavia, survived him for thirty-one years, dying in 1873 aged ninety-five years.

David Morgan-Evans was ordained priest in 1930, so he celebrated his Golden Jubilee in 1980 and his Diamond Jubilee in 1990. The first nine years in the ministry he spent as curate in the parish of Llanryst in St. David's Diocese. His duties there included the Chaplaincy at Gwydyr Castle, seat of the Marquess of Lincolnshire. So it came about that when Lord Carrington, kinsman of the Marquess, needed a Rector of Moulsoe, the young Welsh Curate was invited to London to be interviewed. The interview was to be at Lord Carrington's Club. Getting there was a bit daunting for Morgan whose courage finally failed him in a London taxi. He suddenly panicked at the thought that the cabby might be taking him absolutely *anywhere*. So, when the taxi halted at some traffic lights, he ducked out of it and legged it into Green

Park. The taxi driver's feelings on losing both his client and his fare are not known, but easily imagined. 'And him a parson too!'

Moulsoe, now in Newport Pagnell Deanery, is only in Oxford Diocese by a whisker. Its population is about three hundred, its church basically 13th century with alterations, its Rectory Georgian and enormous. The parish has not been spared the changes common to most villages. The days of fifteen in the choir and sixty plus at Evensong every week are gone. So many other changes too. Morgan-Evans comments, 'There used to be just three cars in the village, mine and two others. Now there are about two hundred'.

If you've been Rector of a small village for nearly half a century you can be forgiven if you sometimes indulge in nostalgia. 'You see that two-acre paddock just beyond the lawn – I used to put that down to potatoes, and I loved to be out there working at five in the morning. First you'd hear the cuckoo, then the school bell, and then the sound of the hammer on the anvil at the smithy.' There are no potatoes planted now – no school bell, and no smithy, but the cuckoo can still be heard in that lovely countryside on the northern edges of Buckinghamshire looking across to the Brickhills.

Little more than ten miles from Moulsoe is the Parish of Emberton. It once had a Rector who served there even longer than Morgan-Evans did at Moulsoe. He was the Reverend Thomas Fry who became Rector of Emberton in 1804 and served the Parish for almost sixty years. A clock tower in the village is his memorial to his wife Margaret.

The Parish of St. James, Great Horwood can boast a 'half-centenarian' Rector. He was the Reverend Simon Thomas Adams, born 1807, died 1889. Of the eighty-two years of his life exactly fifty were spent as Rector of Great Horwood, 1839–1889.

In 1830 Winthrop Mackworth Praed wrote a long poem called 'The Vicar'. It could well serve as a tribute to the long-serving clergy referred to here, and to all the countless other clerics down the centuries who have ministered in small rural communities and ancient village churches.

Here are just five verses from Praed's long poem:

THE VICAR

His talk was like a stream, which runs
With rapid change from rocks to roses;
It slipped from politics to puns,
It passed from Mahomet to Moses;
Beginning with the laws which keep
The planets in their radiant courses,
And ending with some precept deep
For dressing eels, or shoeing horses.

He was a shrewd and sound Divine,
Of loud Dissent the mortal terror;
And when, by dint of page and line,
He 'stablished Truth, or startled Error,
The Baptist found him far too deep;
And the lean Levite went to sleep,
And dreamed of tasting pork tomorrow.

His sermon never said or showed
That Earth is foul, that Heaven is gracious,
Without refreshment on the road
From Jerome, or from Anthanasious;
And sure a righteous Zeal inspired
The head and hand that penned and planned them,
For all who understood admired,
And some who did not understand them.

He did not think all mischief fair,
Although he had a knack for joking;
He did not make himself a bear,
Although he had a taste for smoking;
And when the righteous sects ran made,
He held, in spite of all his learning,
That if a man's belief is bad,
It will not be improved by burning.

And he was kind, and loved to sit
    In the low hut or garnished cottage,
And praise the farmer's homely wit,
    And share the widow's homelier pottage;
At his approach complaint grew mild;
    And when his hand unbarred the shutter,
The clammy lips of fever smiled
    The welcome which they could not utter.

Winthrop Mackworth Praed (1830)

Chapter Nine

DORCHESTER TO OXFORD, VIA WINCHESTER AND LINCOLN

Geographically it is a mere eight miles or so. In terms of diocesan development the distance is somewhat longer!

In 834 St. Berin (or Birinus) led a mission to the West Saxons. He baptised the West Saxon King in the River Thames close to where Dorchester Abbey now stands. Bede, in his Latin 'Historia Ecclesiastica Gentis Anglorum' recorded that, together with Oswald, King of Northumbria, King Cynegils gave Dorchester to be an episcopal see. So Dorchester became a bishopric in the Kingdom of Mercia. The See was later moved to Winchester. However, the seat of the Bishops remained at Dorchester until the Norman Conquest, with jurisdiction extending over the whole of the Midlands as far as, and including, Lincolnshire. In 1072 Lanfranc signed the Charter ordering the See to be moved to Lincoln. That remained the situation for the next four centuries.

In the 16th century Henry VIII embarked on his policy of dissolving the monasteries. A spin-off from this was Henry's decision to create six new Sees, one of which was to be Oxford, taken out of Lincoln. By a Patent on 6th January 1542 Henry VIII provided for the endowment of the new Oxford Diocese, which initially was based at Osney.

In 1546 the seat of the new diocese was removed to the Priory of Saint Frideswide in Oxford itself. Various Manors and desmesnes were added for the funding of the See. In 1547 the young Edward VI granted additional rectories and advowsons to the bishopric. But it was still underfunded and no palace had been appropriated for the bishops.

Dorchester Abbey lost its Cathedral status in 1072. (JH)

Appropriately, the first Bishop of Oxford was Robert King, Suffragan of Lincoln. His episcopacy began in 1542 and lasted till 1558 when he was succeeded by Thomas Goldwell who had been Bishop of St. Asaph. But within a twelvemonth he fled, first to Milan and then to Rome. That was in 1559. Hereafter the Diocese of Oxford proceeded by fits and starts. When Bishop Goldwell fled, the Diocese remained vacant for the next nine years! Then in 1567 Hugh Curwen, the Archbishop of Dublin, became Bishop of Oxford and he did not last long. After his departure the See was vacant again, this time for twenty-one years!

In 1589 John Underhill, Rector of Lincoln College, became bishop, and when he left there was yet another vacancy in the See, this time for eleven years! As the 17th century began things settled down a bit. Bishops Bridges, Howson, Corbet and Bancroft followed in turn – 1604, 1619, 1628 and 1632.

By then Charles I was on the throne. He was pleased to grant Bishop Bancroft and his successors a subvention to assist diocesan finances out of the Royal Forests of Shotover and Stowwood. Licence was also given to unite the Vicarage and Rectory of

Cuddeston and this enabled Bancroft to build an Episcopal Palace at Cuddeston. But this got burnt down in the Civil War and remained a ruin till the Protectorate of Oliver Cromwell ended and the monarchy was restored under Charles II.

The next major development came in 1836 when the whole county of Berkshire was annexed to the Diocese of Oxford. Then on the 19th July 1837 the whole county of Buckinghamshire was similarly annexed to the See by an Order in Council, but this change did not take effect till 1845.

So broadly speaking the Diocese of Oxford came to comprise three whole counties, Oxon., Berks. and Bucks. And each of these forms one of the Archdeaconries into which the Diocese is divided. Looked at another way, the Diocese comprises; the Diocesan Bishop (and as the Millennium began the present Bishop was the forty-first since the Diocese began) along with three Area Bishops – Dorchester, Reading and Buckingham.

So the transition from Dorchester to Oxford was completed. In the years that followed it was often suggested that the Diocese, one of the largest in the country, should perhaps be divided. But this has always been resisted on the grounds, some say, that the River Thames is its unifying feature.

Chapter Ten

SILENCE IN COURT!

In olden times there were always two kinds of Court, secular and clerical. Both existed to exercise discipline. The Church or Ecclesiastical Courts claimed the right to judge the misdemeanours of the clergy and the religious. But they also dealt with the shortcomings of the ordinary folk in the congregations as well. It was accepted that where the sin or fault was public and notorious it should be atoned for by an equally public penance.

A case in point was that of the splendidly named Sir Pexall Brocas. This larger than life character was Lord of the Manor of Little Brickhill. He was notorious as a womaniser and was said to have sired a hundred children. He spent little time in his Manor House, and preferred to live it up in London or elsewhere.

His notoriety finally prompted the Ecclesiastical Court to call him to book. In October 1613 he was found guilty of conduct so scandalous that he was ordered to stand for three days, clad in a white penitential gown, on the steps of St. Paul's Cathedral. He served his penance, but then, being the sort of man he was, he called many of his friends to join him. They all went in a mob, all clad in red, to the Guildhall to demand dinner from the Lord Mayor!

His departure from the world was equally in character. He left a will stipulating that he should have *two* funerals, not one; one in Little Brickhill and the other at Ivinghoe Aston where he also owned land. *And* he left word that part of him should be buried at Little Brickhill and the rest of him at Ivinghoe Aston. The Parish Register makes it clear that his instructions were honoured to the letter, for the Register records that he was 'buried in part' at both places. Which part in which place, one wonders?

* * *

Ecclesiastical boundaries sometimes throw up unexpected results. Thus, in the 16th century it happened that the Archdeaconry of St. Albans included in its jurisdiction four parishes in Buckinghamshire, among them being Winslow. As a result some interesting court cases are included in the ACTA or Records of the St. Albans Archdeaconry. Thus:

'12th September 1584 – Certificate that William Heyres of Wynselow stood in the Church Porch until the First Lesson was ended, in a white sheet, and then came and stood in the Middle Alley, desiring the people to pray for him, and promised amendment of life.'

*

'Certificate that Alse Lockwood, daughter of Harry Lockwood of Wynselow came to the Church and after the Second Lesson stood before the Minister, he reading the Homily against fornication; after the Homily was read, and after saying the Lord's Prayer, she desired the congregation to pray for her, and she did her penance very penitently. 16th Jan: 1586.'

*

'Certificate that Thomas Cowper of Wynselow hath been into the Church and confessed, and was sorry that he had given such offence in the Church, and he would hereafter be better advised. 16th Jan: 1586.'

*

'Anno 1586. Certificate of Vicar, Churchwardens and Sidesmen that Alexander Ward of Wynselow hath been into Church and after the Epistle and Gospel Desired the people to pray to God to forgive him his offence, in that he hath suffered certain persons to be in his house eating and drinking in Service time. 12th March 1586.'
(This person was probably an Innkeeper.)

*

Another entry among the ACTA relates that Robert Dance, Vicar of Winslow, being examined touching his ability of learning and knowledge, for the discharge of his calling in the Ministry, on

4th October 1586, was found to be unable to answer in the Latin tongue, and was able very meanly to satisfy questions of religion in the English tongue.

In the 16th and 17th centuries numbers of the clergy were 'mere readers of prayers' and were often styled 'Reading Vicars' or 'Reading Curates'. In an edition of the Homilies republished in 1562 the Preface stated that 'all they that are appointed Ministers that have *not* the gift of preaching sufficiently to instruct the people' shall read plainly and distinctly one of the said Homilies as they stand in this book'.

*

The fact that Robert Dance, Vicar of Winslow, was subjected to public discipline leads us on to take note of what is often described as 'Benefit of Clergy'. Broadly speaking a clergyman accused of any offence could opt to be tried by an Ecclesiastical Court and not by a secular Court. On the whole punishments were less harsh in Church Courts. And in really serious cases involving an alleged murder a clergyman would certainly benefit to be tried by a Bishops Court, because bishops could not impose the death penalty.

By an Act of Henry VII (1485) 'Benefit of Clergy' was modified. It would still save the neck of a convicted cleric found guilty of murder, but he would not escape altogether. He would be ordered to have his hands branded before release.

Chapter Eleven

KEACH OF WINSLOW

29th February 1640 a son was born to John and Fedora Keeche of Stoke Hammond. They took him to St. Luke's Parish Church to be christened on 6th March. Young Benjamin, who later spelt his name as Keach, grew up in Stoke Hammond. At fifteen he came under the influence of the Arminian Baptists and was baptised again by John Russell, Baptist Minister at Chesham. At nineteen Benjamin Keach began preaching, a truly dangerous thing to do in those days of religious intolerance. At twenty he was appointed Baptist Pastor at Winslow.

A small chapel had been built there in 1625 and it stands there still, probably the oldest nonconformist place of worship in Buckinghamshire, and one of the few remaining Puritan chapels still retaining its original furnishings. The tiny chapel, seating perhaps twenty people on its forms and benches, has a hinged

Keach's Meeting House in Winslow, where Keach ministered from 1660 to 1668. (JH)

shelf against its back wall, serving as a desk on which children were taught to write. Below the pulpit stands the 17th century communion table. On it stands a box containing the pewter communion cup and plate.

Above the pulpit is a memorial tablet commemorating:

'BENJAMIN KEACH *Born 1640 Died 1704*
Pastor of the Baptist Church assembling in this place
from 1660 to 1668, who restored congregation singing of
hymns as a part of Divine Worship and suffered in Prison
and in the Pillory here and at Aylesbury in October 1664
for asserting the right of Liberty and Conscience and
bearing witness to THE SOVEREIGNTY OF CHRIST'.

This records the two great crises of Benjamin's life. First, he suffered at the hands of the establishment. In common with other dissenting preachers of his day, he was hunted down, arrested, tried and imprisoned. This happened halfway through his eight years as Baptist Pastor of Winslow. As well as preaching, he had also published 'A Child's Instructor', a Baptist catechism. At his trial in Aylesbury it was said that this small book 'contained several damnable positions contrary to the Book of Common Prayer and the Liturgy of the Church of England . . . to the great displeasure of God and the King's Peace'. Found guilty, Keach was fined £20 and sent to prison for two weeks. Nor was that all. It was laid down that on the first Saturday of those two weeks he should stand in the pillory at Aylesbury, and on the second Thursday in the pillory at Winslow, where his book should be burnt before his eyes by the common hangman. On both occasions, as soon as his head was fixed in the pillory, the unrepentant Keach preached to the onlookers.

After eight years at Winslow, Keach sold up and left for London with his family. The coach was waylaid by highwaymen who robbed them of everything. For the remaining thirty years of his life he exercised his ministry as a Baptist preacher in London. The Indulgence of 1672 made life easier for dissenting preachers, but Keach later faced opposition from a different quarter – his own Baptist Church. In 1688 he introduced congregational

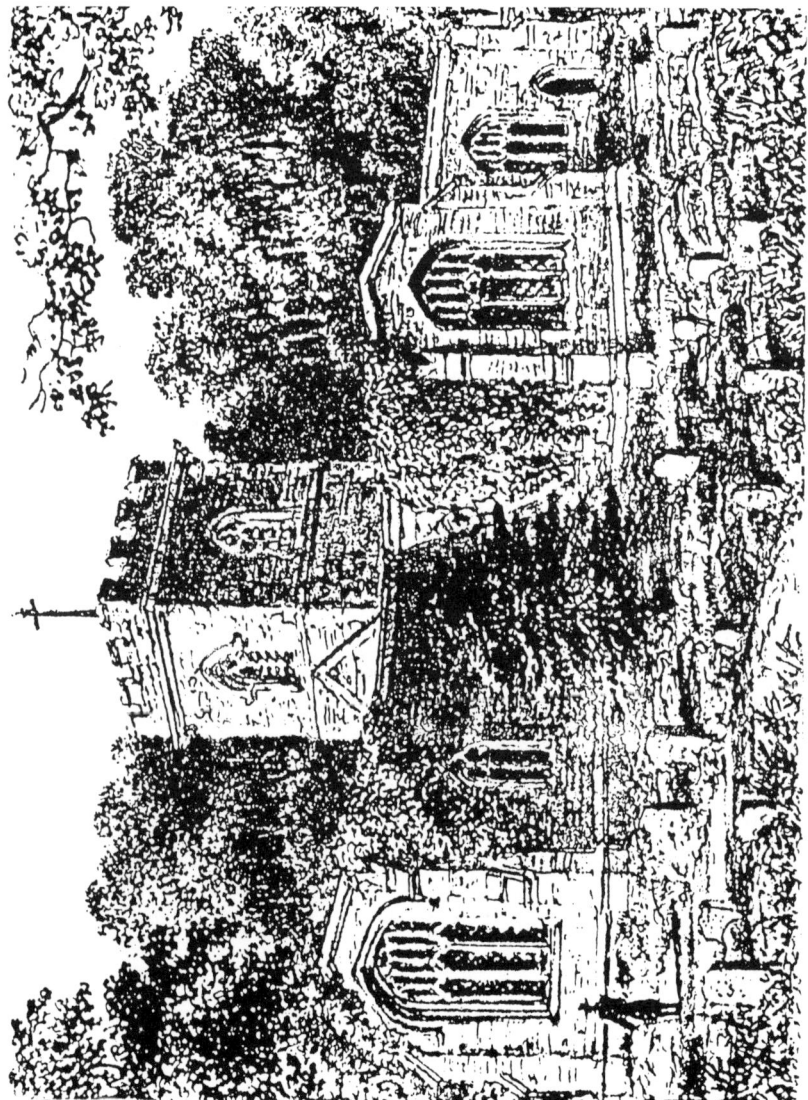

St. Luke's Church, Stoke Hammond, where Keach was christened in 1640.

Keach in the stocks – still preaching!

hymn-singing at the chapel in Goat Yard Passage, Horsleydown. This brought down on his head the wrath of the London General Baptist Association which, in 1689, condemned the practice as 'carnal formality'. Keach refused to desist and in 1691 published a collection of original hymns, but the issue split the congregation.

He married twice, and five daughters were born to each wife. His first wife also bore him a son, who followed his father into the Baptist ministry, and served both in Pennsylvania and in London.

Benjamin Keach died in 1704 and was buried in Southwark. Although he was Pastor of the little chapel in Winslow for only eight of the more than three hundred and sixty years that the chapel has stood there, his spirit seems still to pervade it, and it is known to everyone as Keach's Meeting House. Down the years it has been lovingly maintained; its Trustees are to be commended and should surely be helped to keep this moving little piece of Bucks history in good repair.

Chapter Twelve

WATER STRATFORD'S ARMAGEDDON, THE OBSESSION OF JOHN MASON

Actually, he had two obsessions, one after the other. The dictionary defines Obsession as 'a persistent idea or impulse; a persistent idea or feeling, sometimes akin to madness'.

John Mason came to Water Stratford as Vicar in 1674 and stayed there till he died in 1694. Both he and his wife were popular. The Vicar loved hymn-writing and the villagers appreciated the fame that his hymns earned for the parish. John Mason was a great student of the Bible, and therein lay his first obsession. He was convinced that through the chronology of Scripture he could determine the whole history of the world and trace it back to the exact date of creation.

He wasn't the first to have such ideas. Before him there had been James Ussher, an Anglican Bishop of the Church of Ireland. He too believed that by taking the individuals and events recorded in the Bible, and assigning dates to them, you could, by working backwards, arrive at Genesis Chapter One, and be able to state with authority exactly when God created the world. And that date, declared Bishop Ussher, was precisely the year 4004BC!

Bishop Ussher died in 1656, eighteen years before John Mason became Vicar of Water Stratford. Mason undoubtedly knew of Bishop Ussher's work but he didn't agree with his findings. So he worked on his own and reached his own conclusions. His labours were truly obsessive. At last he announced his results. And he was shattered when nobody took any notice! The Church rejected his theories and his findings. So all those years of study had been in vain. He was heart-broken and mortified.

Coincidentally, his wife died just at that time. John Mason's world collapsed about him. He suffered nightmares and horrifying dreams He carried on as Vicar of Water Stratford but in a sort of daze. The double blows he had suffered had driven him into a sort of madness.

His first obsession, trying to establish how and when the world began, was now abandoned. And his mind now turned in the opposite direction. His second obsession took possession of him. He would study the matter of the end of the world, and discover when and how it would come about. He worked as frenetically on this anticipation of the coming day of Judgement as once he had worked on tracing the origins of the world and its creation.

He reached some astonishing conclusions! He ended by announcing not only that he knew precisely when the Day of Judgement would come, but also, more astonishingly, that when Judgement Day came, only Water Stratford would be saved and all the rest would be lost!

Hellfire preaching along these lines drew crowds from far and wide. So effective was this preaching that people from far away sold their property and moved to Water Stratford, determined to be in that one small place which the Vicar said would survive the Day of Judgement.

Water Stratford Church, scene of astonishing events in 1693. (JH)

Browne Willis wrote about this strange Rector of Water Stratford in his 'History of Buckingham' published in 1755. He wrote:

> 'In the years 1693 and 1694, this place was much resorted unto on account its Rector, Mr John Mason, who taught publicly that he had seen Christ, and that he had at this place begun His Personal reign on earth; which enthusiastical predictions occasioned great resort hither from many parts of the neighbourhood insomuch that all the Barns and Houses hereabouts were filled with his followers, many of whom were so infatuated that they sold their estates, being persuaded that this World was at an end; and so took up their abodes and dwelt here some years after his death'.

We have an interesting contemporary comment on all this in the shape of a letter written in 1694 by a gentleman who lived near Water Stratford to his brother in London, he wrote:

> 'Brother, I have here according to your desire, sent an account concerning Mr Mason, Minister of Water Stratford. I have heard some of his hearers say that they did believe they should see Christ appear, but in what manner they would not be positive. Some of them would say visibly appear: others say his appearance in the clouds & his reign in the clouds. Further, I have heard them say that those who did not believe this, and did see his appearance would live one thousand years, and all that while without sin; and likewise that the fulness of the Gentiles was come in. They call Water Stratford SION, and count Mr Mason a prophet in whom alone the revelations of St. John will be revealed. They do conclude their reign will begin about Ascension Day next; and that all that believe this must dwell at Water Stratford and there they will be preserved; and neither magistrate can meddle with them, nor any other hurt can befall them, and that they shall stand upon Mount Sion, and see all the wicked round about them be burnt up. They have had musick & dancing & singing of hymns & clapping of hands, about 6 weeks night & day. The week before Easter several families moved to Water Stratford to live, carrying all they had thither. They sold houses and land for what they could get. They did, last winter, lay in at Stratford 20 quarters of wheat, 10 quarters of malt & 20 or 30 hundred weight of cheese. This spring they have laid in several fat bullocks & hogs.

'On Easter Monday night Mr Mason declares he saw Christ, and on the next Lord's Day following some of our neighbours went to Stratford to hear and see how the people went on; and being a great multitude of people gathered together round the country, more than the church could contain, they stood in the minister's yard, and he, out of his chamber window, declared unto the multitude that on the Monday night before, he being in bed and awake, lying on his left side, he turned himself to his right and saw Christ sitting in a chair, and a candle lighted in a candle-stick standing on a stool; and that Christ was clothed in a purple robe, dipped in the blood of his enemies. He confirmed this with an oath, saying by the eternal God that what he said was true, and that himself was neither in a dream, nor mad or drunken and neither was affrighted.

He hath not given the sacraments these last 2 years, and now they do not read nor pray, only 4 or 5 of the last words of the Lord's Prayer, which is in the praise of the glory of God. They say all is done and there is nothing to be done, only to praise God. There may be about 40 that are constant, but there are sometimes about 500 or 1000 to see their fashions and actions in dancing.

'Your brothers & some other young men went last Saturday night to see them and stayed all night. The dancing is in no order but after an antic manner, sometimes 3 taking hand & jumping round; others leaping from one end of the room to the other, catching over their heads with their hands, and clapping them saying, sometimes, appear, appear, appear, while others say glory, glory, glory.

There is one dancer among them with a wooden leg and he makes great noise among them with his leg when he cuts capers. Mr Mason will not dispute with any divine concerning his opinions but will only say all is done; they that are righteous, let them be righteous still; and they that are filthy; let them be filthy still. Divers ministers go to see him, and in particular our Minister, Mr Crofts, who went last Sunday but could not be admitted to see Mr Mason, he then being ill with a quinsie.

(But Mr Croft talked with) some of the hearers, in particular the man with the wooden leg. Mr Croft said that the heavens must retain Christ until the restitution of all things. The man said all *things ARE restored, but our minister answered they are not all restored, because he had not got his good leg restored again.*

We do hear that within the past two days some of the saints of this new-named Sion have left it and go about their employment again. I know no more at present, but when I am further satisfied of their proceedings you shall know of it. Yours, etc.'

What were the Church authorities doing about all this? They were naturally alarmed, but were at a loss to know how to handle it. They decided to send a senior clergyman to look into the matter and report. The man they chose was the Reverend Maurice, Rector of Tyringham. Maurice had been a friend of John Mason for the past twenty years. So it was thought that he would be welcomed, and yet sufficiently detached to make a mature assessment.

Maurice was astonished and appalled at what he found. All over the village, but most of all in and around the Church, he found crowds, dancing, singing, clapping, in a state of high hysteria, determined to be ready when Judgement Day should come.

He made his way to the Vicarage and things there were even more chaotic. People were swarming in and out of the house and up and down the stairs. The noise of their singing and chanting was deafening. Some of them danced and sang so exuberantly that they dropped exhausted. But others took their place and the frenetic singing and dancing continued unabated.

Meanwhile, at the very top of the house in an attic, the Vicar lay dying. His sister, who was at his bedside, explained to Maurice that her brother had been struck dumb. He could hear but not speak. She begged Maurice not to distress her brother by questioning him about recent happenings in the village. That was all very well, but Maurice had been sent to assess the situation and would have to give a report to his superiors. He tried to question others in the house, but no real dialogue was possible. People simply told him that he was damned and should leave.

A month later, in 1694, the Reverend John Mason died. He had often told people that though he might die, he would be resurrected after three days. It was said by some that this had actually happened, and that they had seen him.

The church authorities sent a replacement for John Mason. The new Vicar, a man named Rushworth, cannot have relished his appointment. Faced with those repeated tales about a resurrected John Mason having been seen, Rushworth went to the length of opening up the grave to demonstrate to all that the body of the dead John Mason was still there.

The crowds for the most part dispersed, and life in Water Stratford returned to a semblance of normality. But a few people, who had come from elsewhere, stayed on. They still believed that the late John Mason had been right, and that only in Water Stratford would they be safe when Judgement Day came. Some of them were still there sixteen years after John's death.

Long before that the Reverend Maurice had reported back to his superiors. It was a fair and charitable report. Maurice was at pains to stress his conviction that John Mason had genuinely believed that his village and parish had been specially set apart by God. But if this was but a delusion, Maurice had tried to find an explanation for it. And he was satisfied that he had found one. John Mason's delusion, he said, had been brought about by his addiction to tobacco! Whenever he had visited his friend over the years he had always found him enveloped in clouds of smoke. Clearly, he concluded, this had overheated John's brain.

But perhaps the poet, Alexander Pope, would have been nearer the mark with his line:

'A little learning is a dang'rous thing'.

Chapter Thirteen

COLE VERSUS LEYCESTER, FENNY STRATFORD

Browne Willis, as Lord of the Manors of Whaddon, Bletchley, and Fenny Stratford, had the right to appoint the clergy in the parishes of both Bletchley and Fenny Stratford. In the case of the latter he had especial right.

There was much of the autocrat in Browne Willis, and he had fixed ideas about how things should be done. For the most part he got his own way – but not always. For example, he laid down that any Priest he appointed to the Parish of Fenny Stratford should be:

'a graduate of either Oxford or Cambridge
unmarried
a "native of South Britain"
and willing to reside in the Parish'.

The first man he appointed, the Reverend Samuel Clark, fitted the bill admirably on three of four counts. He was a graduate, MA Oriel College, Oxford; he was an Englishman; he was happy to reside in the parish. But he decided to get married, and did in fact marry the sister of the Curate of Simpson. He felt obliged to keep his wife in London so that Browne Willis should not learn of his married status.

Another matter on which Browne Willis had decided views concerned the calendar. In 1752 it was decided to change the calendar in Britain to bring it into line with Europe. This meant an adjustment of eleven days. In other words, what had been the 15th day of the month would become the 4th of the month, and so on. The conservative Browne Willis was furious and wanted no truck with the new calendar. He wasn't alone. In some places people rioted and loudly demanded, 'Give us back our eleven days!'

The North East Prospect of
St. Martins Chapel at
Fenny Stratford.

St. Martin's Church, Fenny Stratford as Browne Willis built it in 1730.
It has twice been extended since then.

What particularly incensed Browne Willis is that, whereas
St. Martin's Day had always been 22nd November, now it was to
be 11th November. He had decided views on how that day should
be celebrated each year. There should be a service in Church with
a special preacher; a special lunch or dinner; and the three-fold
firing of the Fenny Poppers. And as long as Browne Willis had
any say in the matter, all this should take place on what he
regarded as the proper day for Martinmas – 22nd November. This
uncertainty whether the new or the old calendar was being followed
was to lead to endless confusion, not least in the controversy that
was to follow – the Cole versus Leycester saga.

In February 1760 Browne Willis died and was buried in his
beloved St. Martin's. In the following year it fell to the Reverend
William Cole, Rector of St. Mary's, Bletchley, to appoint a new
Priest for St. Martin's, Fenny Stratford. He chose the Reverend
Ralph Leycester, a choice he was later to regret.

If Samuel Clark had scored three out of four on the Browne Willis scale, Ralph Leycester scored only two. He was an Oxford graduate and he was an Englishman. But he was determined to live at Heath and Reach, not in his parish at Fenny. And he married, taking as bride the sister of Sir Walden Hanmer, Lord of the Manor of Simpson.

Cole and Leycester never got on well together. And one of the first things they quarrelled about was that tiresome business of the new calendar, and whether Martinmas should be kept on the new or the old date.

In 1763 Cole wrote to Mr Cooke of Water Eaton, the Steward for the Lord of the Manor, and asked him to see that St. Martin's Day should be celebrated as usual. On the new-style calendar that would be on 11th November. But unfortunately a great flood (common in those days) had cut all communications between Fenny Stratford and Water Eaton. So it was decided to keep the festival on the old-style date, i.e. 22nd November when the floods had receded. But again difficulties arose. There was an outbreak of smallpox in Fenny Stratford and people were reluctant to attend St. Martin's Church. So the St. Martin's Day service was held at Bletchley instead of at Fenny. And the customary dinner was held at a Bletchley inn, instead of at the Bull in Fenny. Ralph Leycester was highly indignant and said loudly and publicly that it was just as well the service had been at Bletchley because he would not have allowed them in St. Martin's Church in any case.

There was similar trouble in 1765. The 11th November that year was a Sunday. So Cole announced that Martinmas would be celebrated on the Monday, 12th November. He sent a message to this effect to Ralph Leycester and asked him to see that St. Martin's Church would be open at 11am on the Monday. And he invited Leycester to join the company for dinner afterwards at the Bull. Ralph Leycester replied to that letter in sharp terms on the Sunday, 11th November. He wrote that the people of Fenny were angry at the suggestion that the service and the dinner should be on Monday 12th November when everybody knew that 22nd November was the proper day for both!

Cole replied temperately. He said he did not mind whether they followed the old calendar or the new – one day was as good as another. But it was too late now to change the arrangements already made. All the guests for both service and dinner had already been invited. So, please, make sure the Church is opened at 11am tomorrow.

Next morning, Monday 12th November Cole went to Fenny. He found St. Martin's Church locked and was told the keys had been taken to Heath and Reach. Not to be outdone, Cole managed to open a window and put somebody into the Church to open it from the inside. He then conducted the service at which he preached. After church the guests repaired to the nearby Bull Inn for the customary dinner. Leycester had not attended the service not did he come to the dinner. Instead, he stayed outside in the inn yard, shouting abuse at Cole and his guests.

All this was too much for Cole and he wrote a long complaint about Leycester to the Bishop of Lincoln. In it he described Leycester's uncouth behaviour, and he also mentioned that, for three years running, Leycester had collected funds for holding a

Cole once called Fenny Stratford 'the sink of all that is bad'.

second St. Martin's Day on the old date, 22nd November, even though Cole had already seen to the observance on the new-style date, 11th November.

There were other grounds for complaint. Leycester persisted in living at Heath and Reach instead of in the Parish. And he had unlawfully cut down twenty-nine trees on the Church's glebe lands.

To Cole's disappointment the Bishop took no action. So Cole wrote again, repeating the original complaints and adding new ones. He told the Bishop, for example, that on 6th January 1765 the bells at St. Martin's rang for so long waiting for Leycester to arrive to take the service, that the ringers gave up, exhausted. And inside the Church the choir got so tired filling in with psalm-singing that they had to go out for gin before coming back into Church to sing yet more psalms! And in the end Leycester never did arrive that day, or send any excuse or explanation for his absence.

No doubt the Bishop did eventually take some action and suggest that Leycester should mend his ways. But he certainly did not remove him. In fact Leycester stayed on for years, outlasting Cole. Cole left Bletchley in 1767, but Leycester stayed to the end of the century. In 1793 a later Bishop of Lincoln appointed him as Rector of Hedsor. He died in 1803.

Chapter Fourteen

THE ODD SHILLING, FENNY STRATFORD

The Reverend Maurice Wheeler did not like what happened to him that day in Fenny Stratford in the year 1710. He was a dignified figure, this distinguished cleric, aged about sixty-two. Until two years before he had been Master of Gloucester Cathedral School. He was, besides, a Prebendary of Lincoln. At the time of the unfortunate incident in Fenny Stratford he was Rector of Wappenham in Northamptonshire. History does not relate where he was coming from or going to when he rode through Fenny Stratford, but we have his own testimony about what befell him.

To be fair to Fenny, and to be more accurate, the indignity to his person happened at Simpson rather than at Fenny itself. Posterity might never have learned about the affair were it not for the fact that in 1725 the good burgesses of Fenny Stratford published a circular letter in a newspaper. And they sent copies of it also to a number of parishes. The circular had actually been composed by Browne Willis and some thirty prominent citizens signed it. It related how 'our town, which is an ancient Market Town, and great thoroughfare from London to Chester and Ireland, lies at least one mile from our Mother Church'. It went on to say that because of this a new church was being built in Fenny Stratford. The tower was already finished, and the walls were up to ten feet. Now help was needed to finish the work and the circular letter solicited donations. It met with a far response, some twenty-one parishes replying.

Among them was the Parish of Wappenham, where the good Prebendary Wheeler was Rector. When he received the circular his mind went back to that day, some fifteen years before, when he

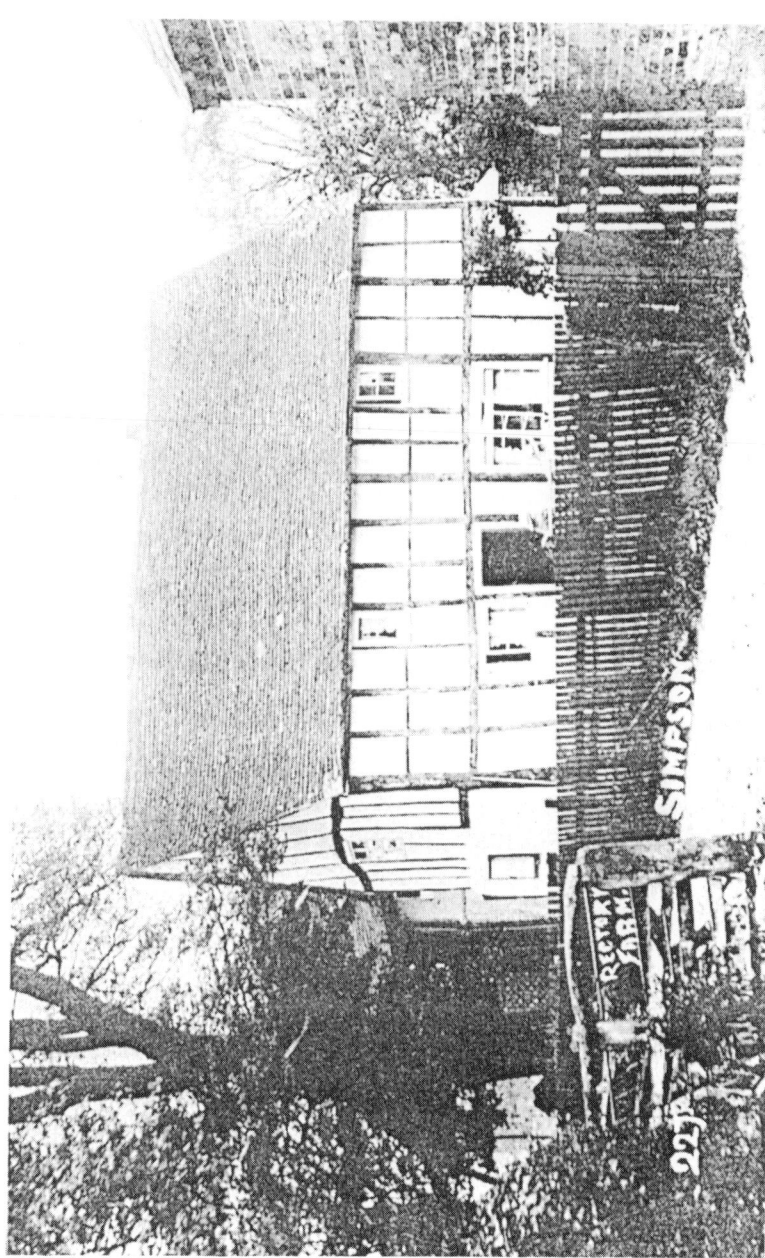

The Rectory Farm at Simpson village, where Prebendary Wheeler suffered his indignity in 1710.

had been so unceremoniously treated as he rode through Fenny Stratford. A lesser man might have thrown the Appeal on the fire. But not the good Prebendary. He decided to send a donation, and to use the occasion to administer a rebuke.

So what was it that had happened all those years before? Well, as he rode through Fenny that day, back in 1710, he had sand thrown in his face. He decided to send a donation of one guinea, and in his letter he wrote: 'Twenty shillings is towards the building, and the odd shilling is given upon a very odd occasion, towards cleaning the chapel, when finished, of chips, dust and rubbish, and in remembrance of my cleaning my own face when dashed with grains as I was passing through the place'.

The memory of that long-ago incident must have come back to him as he wrote this letter, because he went on: 'A rudeness anything like this having not anywhere met with in my whole life, but at Fenny, I cannot easily forget, nor did I remember it now with any other resentment than as done to a clergyman; though had the people been some of the most ill-bred brutes of the earth, yet their subsistence being wholly by travellers might (one would think) have in point of interest put so much sense into their heads as to be civil to strangers in any garb, at least not to be abusive to a clergyman'.

No doubt feeling better for having got that off his chest, he concluded his letter in calmer vein: 'Religion teaches civility and good manners towards man, as well as piety and devotion towards God, and I hope the erecting of this chapel among them may in good time have this visible effect upon the inhabitants, as in both respects to reform them'.

Chapter Fifteen

A VIGIL AT QUAINTON –
ELEVEN DAYS OF CHRISTMAS

'Twas the night before Christmas . . .'

With those immortal words Charles Dickens began one of his most popular stories. The same words can be the opening for *this* story too, a story that belongs to a time about a century before Dickens, and set not in London but in Quainton.

It is Christmas Eve, 1753. Or is it?

That is what some two thousand people are wondering. They are crowded into the Rector's garden in Quainton, with torches and lanterns. They have come not only from Quainton but also from a dozen villages roundabout – from North Marston and Granborough, from Oving and Waddesdon, from Whitchurch and even from Winslow. There is excitement and much pushing and shoving. And then, as midnight approaches, the hubbub dies down and lanterns are raised even higher, as people press forward for a better view.

Why are they there? What do they expect to happen?

To answer those questions you must go back twice into the past. First, into the very recent past, just to last year, 1752. In that year, by Statute 24 of George II it was decreed Britain would change its calendar to bring these islands into line with the continent of Europe. The old Julian calendar would be dropped and the Gregorian calendar would henceforth be followed. To make the change-over it was announced that 24th September 1752, would be followed *next day* by 14th September.

There was consternation everywhere. People thought they were being cheated out of eleven days of their lives – and that their life-spans would be shortened by nearly two weeks! And would it not mean that they were being cheated out of eleven days' pay? There were near-riots in many places, and the cry went up all over the land: 'Give us back our eleven days!'

Quainton and its surrounding villages were as much affected by all this furore as anywhere else in the country. Here, as elsewhere, the arguments waxed vehemently.

History does not relate who first suggested the idea that the argument might be settled in Quainton. Quainton had something that could resolve the doubts and settle the argument. To know what that 'something' was means a second going back into the past. A long way back this time – to AD63 in fact.

In AD63, so folklore and fable said, Joseph of Arimathea came to Britain and so brought the Christian faith. He settled in Glastonbury. And he did not come empty-handed. Folklore and fable said that he brought with him the Holy Grail, the very Cup that Christ had used at the Last Supper. He also brought his staff and planted it in the soil in Glastonbury. Miraculously, the staff took root and grew into a tree. And the tree miraculously budded and flowered every Christmas in honour of Christ's birth. It was widely believed that the Glastonbury Thorn flowered at midnight on Christmas Eve, and that the blossoms lasted just the one day – the day of the Saviour's birth.

And Quainton comes into the picture because in the Rector's garden there was a tree said to have been grown from a cutting from the famous Glastonbury Thorn Tree. That's why the crowd had gathered. They hoped that their own local descendant from the Glastonbury Thorn Tree could settle their doubts once and for all. They would trust nature to decide for them whether tomorrow, 25th December 1753 (new style) was Christmas Day or not. If the thorn tree in the Rector's garden showed signs of budding on the 24th December (new style) then they would accept that both by the Law of the Land and the Law of Nature next day really would be Christmas Day.

Came midnight – and no buds appeared.

The crowd lingered for a while, to give the tree a chance. But no buds appeared. 'That's it, then,' they said, 'tomorrow isn't a true and proper Christmas Day, no matter what the King and his

Parliament may say'. And they all went home.

So on Christmas Day 1753 (new style) nobody went to Church in Quainton, and there were no Christmas festivities. Instead, eleven days later, people kept Christmas Day on the old date of the 5th January.

In time, of course, the fuss died down – the new calendar was gradually accepted by everyone and Christmas Day was accepted to be the 25th December.

But, for the record, 5th January, which on the Julian calendar is Old Christmas Day, has for centuries been called Twelfth Night. It is the eve of the twelfth day after Christmas. And that twelfth day is Feast of the Epiphany, which celebrates the coming to Bethlehem of the Three Wise Men.

So, whether in Quainton or anywhere else, the Christmas festival neatly spans the eleven days that everyone got so worked up about nearly two and a half centuries ago.

(This chapter first appeared in 'Tales from Milton Keynes'
by John Houghton.)

Chapter Sixteen

THE MAD MONKS OF MEDMENHAM
SCANDAL AT WEST WYCOMBE!

Hugh de Bolebec founded the Cistercian Abbey at Woburn in the year 1200. An offshoot or cell of the Abbey was later set up at Medmenham on the banks of the Thames about four miles from Henley. So the first Monks of Medmenham were there in the 13th century. By the early 16th century Medmenham Priory was annexed to Bisham Abbey on the other side of the river.

At the Reformation all monasteries and priories, including Medmenham, were closed. The Priory then fell into disrepair after the Monks had been turned out. They had never enjoyed any great reputation for piety and were described by some as 'lawless'.

Some two hundred years later there would be other 'monks' at Medmenham, bogus monks, members of the Hell Fire Club, and *their* reputation would be infinitely more questionable!

SIR FRANCIS DASHWOOD

Sir Francis Dashwood was born in 1708. When he was sixteen his father died and he inherited a considerable fortune. He also inherited West Wycombe House and spent much effort and money to develop the grounds to the attractive high standards they still maintain today.

Nearby were the ruins of the old Medmenham Abbey, and it occurred to Sir Francis that they might make a splendid setting for a fantastic plan he had in mind. The original Abbey had been home for the monks of long ago. Well then, he would bring monks back to Medmenham!

Sir Francis was an eccentric. After travel in Italy he had returned to England and, with other wealthy friends who had also travelled in Italy, he founded the Society of the Dilettanti, a dining society exclusively for gentlemen of wealth and position interested in fine arts and all things Italian.

He had entered Parliament in 1741, and in about 1745 he had this eccentric notion – bringing monks once more back to Medmenham! From Francis Duffield he acquired the lease of the old Abbey ruins and he announced the foundation of 'The Brotherhood of Saint Francis of Wycombe', with himself as St. Francis of Wycombe!

So began the brief but startling history of 'the mad monks of Medmenham'. They probably never numbered more than thirteen at any one time but they were all men of rank and position. The membership included Lord Melcombe, the Earl of Sandwich, William Hogarth the artist, Charles Churchill, a poet and former priest, Frederick Prince of Wales, John Wilkes, and Paul Whitehead, the satirist and minor poet, who was treasurer. Together the mad monks of Medmenham were members of The Hell Fire Club.

The 'monks' of the mock order used pseudonyms. They wore white habits, but the 'Prior' sported a red bonnet. For their entertainment mock 'nuns' were brought down from London. Inevitably stories spread of shocking goings-on at Medmenham! The word 'orgy' sprang to many people's lips. And even if the stories were exaggerated, there can be little doubt that they were not without foundation.

The heyday of the Mad Monks of Medmenham lasted from 1745 to 1763. Their founder, Sir Francis Dashwood, had already been an MP since 1741. From 1761 to 1762 he was Chancellor of the Exchequer no less, and thereafter Postmaster General from 1766 to 1781. It might seem surprising then that he, and other notable persons who were members of The Hell Fire Club, should be able to combine high public office with such private behaviour. But the fact is that rakish behaviour was a feature of 18th century social life for many. And it could well be that what went on at Medmenham was never as outrageous as many supposed. The stories grew in the telling.

This was certainly the view of Dr Benjamin Bates of Little Missenden. He was himself a member of The Hell Fire Club and was personal physician to Sir Francis Dashwood. He lived to the ripe old age of ninety-eight, dying in 1828. He maintained to the end that people should not credit all they heard about the Mad Monks of Medmenham.

THE GOLDEN BALL

Throughout this period Sir Francis continued to take seriously his duties as a great landowner. The surroundings of West Wycombe House and of the Abbey ruins themselves continued to be developed and beautified. He rebuilt West Wycombe Church, but here too his eccentricity played a part. He built it at the top of a hill and in its tower he set a great golden ball. This glistens in the sun and gives the church tower a unique feature. Just how unique can be appreciated when one learns that the golden ball is large enough to accommodate six or more people. And it often did so. John Wilkes testifies that he took part in a drinks party inside the golden ball with several members of The Hell Fire Club. 'The best Globe Tavern I ever was in' he boasted.

As a conscientious landowner and employer Francis Dashwood (who succeeded to the title of 15th Baron Le Despencer in 1762) embarked on a great road building scheme which would both benefit the neighbourhood and provide jobs for many. For this he needed huge quantities of roadmaking material. He found this ready to hand in the caves of the steep West Wycombe hill, from which his employees extracted all the material they needed.

John Wilkes and several other 'Mad Monks of Medmenham' held a drinks party inside the Golden Ball on West Wycombe Church tower.

This exercise considerably extended, widened and deepened the caves which were already there. It then occurred to him that these caves would make a more exciting, and less public, venue for the meetings of The Hell Fire Club. Thereafter such meetings took place in the caves.

THE SATANIC BABOON

Many are the tales told of those meetings. They figured in a novel, called Chrysal, written in the 1760s by Charles Johnstone. One such tale relates how a baboon was introduced to impersonate Satan. This landed on the shoulder of Lord Sandwich and so terrified him that he fled screaming from the caves.

The Hell Fire Club had a motto – *'Fay ce que vous voudras'*. This is only half of the full original version. 'Do as you like' was the Hell Fire Club motto. The full version is: 'Do as you like – *and pay for it!'*

On the whole the Mad Monks of Medmenham and their Hell Fire Club have had a bad press. Perhaps they deserved it. Certainly most references to them in later accounts have been couched in reproving, moralistic language. Thus, Brewer's Dictionary of Phrase and Fable writes of the 'profanities' at Medmenham. E S Roscoe, in his book, Buckinghamshire, published in 1903, writes: 'Their form of amusement was at once profane and childish, mimicking as they did religious rites in their social meetings.' In fairness, Roscoe did add: 'but the character of their gatherings was probably neither better nor worse than that of others before or since'. But then he spoils this seeming fairness and even-handedness by continuing: 'From the positions of those who took part they have achieved a disagreeable fame'.

Hell Fire Club members, perhaps, would have accepted that. 'We did what we liked – and we don't mind paying for it'.

(This chapter first appeared in 'Eccentrics and Villains, Hauntings and Heroes' by John Houghton.)

131

Chapter Seventeen

THE COUNTIES MERGED – EATON BRAY WITH EDLESBOROUGH

This book has been a Miscellany – a collection or sampling of tales, events and persons which tells of sanctity and scandal in our neighbouring counties of Beds and Bucks. Ecclesiastically, the book has for the most part been concerned with the once huge diocese of Lincoln. But in the past couple of centuries there emerged the dioceses of St. Albans and Oxford. The former is largely co-terminus with Bedfordshire; the latter covers three counties of which Bucks is one.

It made sense to search for sanctity and scandal separately – in Beds or in Bucks. But there exists one small area where such clear-cut divisions are merged. In 1945 Eaton Bray and Edlesborough were merged into one ecclesiastical parish. The former is in the county of Bedfordshire and the latter is in Buckinghamshire. The merged parish is in the diocese of St. Albans, notwithstanding Edlesborough's history in Bucks, and its former parish life in the diocese of Oxford.

So by way of a Postscript, let us see what this 'hybrid' parish of Eaton Bray with Edlesborough has to show us of sanctity and scandal.

EATON BRAY

Take Eaton Bray first. The church of St. Mary the Virgin dates back to the 13th century. But in the middle of the 19th century it was in a terrible state. The Northampton Mercury of February 8th 1847 reported as follows:

'The usual plastering has done much towards obscuring all the beautiful ornaments which may be found here. Two pews are

St. Mary The Virgin, Eaton Bray.

stuffed into the chancel. There is a very common altar-table. The floor is paved with tiles fit only for a barn or scullery. Shouldering the pulpit is a coal cellar. A stove has a chimney shaft piercing the roof. And the fireplace was left in a state that we believe the humblest of the congregation would not suffer in his own cottage. Some tins, dirty with tallow grease, indicate the folly of shutting out the light from the west, which was most clumsily effected by an organ, with some ugly boards, painted black'.

Clearly nothing was done to correct this scandalous state of affairs, for in 1872 the architect, Robert Edis, commented:

'I have never seen a church so utterly neglected, in such a shameful state of decay and dilapidation, or one which could more fairly be said to be an utter disgrace to the religious enlightenment and feeling of the 19th century'.

In 1871 the Revd. John Doe became Vicar and served as such for twenty years. Because the church itself was in such a parlous state, services were moved to the Schoolhouse from 1875 to 1884.

Very slowly, the work of renovating the church began. Sadly in 1880 a workman was killed by a fall of stone from the tower.

Meanwhile, all was far from well in the parish itself. John Doe managed to quarrel with almost everyone. He busied himself with breeding pigs and raising ducks. He offered his services to act as village dentist. But it was his 'high church' ways which gave most offence. 'Call me Father Doe,' he insisted. His time as Vicar came to an abrupt end in 1890. He was in the pulpit preaching one Sunday when he suddenly 'blew his top'. He tore off his surplice and flung it into the congregation! Then he announced that he was to become a Roman Catholic. He climbed out of the pulpit, stormed out of church and subsequently left the parish.

To offset this scandal it is good to pay tribute to Doe's successor, Edwin Sutton. His energetic approach to the restoration of the church began in 1891. It took until 1916 for the work to be completed. As any who visit the church today can see, the restoration was carried out with skill and sensitivity, reflecting great credit on all concerned. So it was a glad day, September 2nd 1916, when the Bishop of St. Albans dedicated the restored church.

By 1970 further maintenance was needed. Ten years' more work restored all the stonework, and all the corbels and the side Chapel reredos were beautifully painted. The festival of thanksgiving which followed included a Flower Festival. Garlands of flowers hung high in the roof, and for these nylon cords were needed. The problem of getting the nylon cords over the roof beams was neatly solved – they called in the help of England's only professional archer, who lived in nearby Leighton Buzzard, and he shot the cords over the beams with consummate ease.

This and much else of interest is related in the excellent Guide Book at the church, edited by Margaret Jones.

EDLESBOROUGH

Meanwhile, what of Edlesborough? What has it to tell us of sanctity or scandal?

The great Bucks historian, George Lipscomb, wrote in 1847 of Edlesborough that it was one of the most extensive parishes in the area – sixteen miles in circumference. Its boundaries touched on

Hertfordshire to the south; on Bedfordshire to the north; while it was itself in the county of Buckinghamshire. For all its size, its population was relatively small. In the century from 1801 to 1901 it grew only from 997 to 1099 and by 1921 was down to 898.

The Church Registers and Records date back to 1567. An ecclesiastical census carried out in 1851 all over England was asked to record attendances at all places of worship. For St. Mary the Virgin, Edlesborough, these revealed attendances on Sunday as follows: fifty on Sunday morning, plus one hundred and seventy Morning Scholars and two hundred on Sunday afternoon, plus one hundred and seventy Afternoon Sunday Scholars. All this suggests sanctity rather than scandal! So far so good.

The Church, a handsome Gothic structure, is notable for its splendid position, high up on a hill, which looks as if it might have been an ancient fortress. the church originally belonged to the Monks of Charterhouse. The various Manors in the parish belonged to a range of owners, frequently changing after the Reformation.

St. Mary the Virgin, Edlesborough.

Brasses in the church record some of them. One of the manors was part of the estate of Thomas Chaucer, son of the poet. Alice Chaucer brought it in marriage to William De La Pole, Duke of Suffolk. His son, John, gave it to the Dean and Chapter of Windsor, with the King's Licence in 1480.

The parish register records the burial of Michael Fenn at the great age of one hundred and twenty four on April 21st 1675. Such longevity surely indicates sanctity and an absence of scandal! But scandal was not entirely absent, as witness the murder of a gardener, killed in a brawl between rival households. His ghost, they say, is sometimes seen in the grounds of the Old Vicarage. Then there was Jack the Leather also known as 'Old Leather Breeches'. His ghost too is often mentioned. Whether or not the ghost stories can be believed, it is certainly a fact that he was a reprobate, a highwayman who was dragged from his hiding place in the farm stables and carried off the the gibbet at Ivinghoe Beacon.

In the Church there is the unique Rose Brass. Its wording seems to be a sort of riddle, though whether its answer has anything to tell us about either sanctity or scandal you must judge for yourself. The wording of the brass says:

'What I spent I had,
What I gave I have,
What I refused I am being punished for,
What I kept I have lost'.

What does it mean? Answers on a postcard, please.

Edlesborough Church is redundant now and is cared for by the Churches Conservation Trust, which has spent much money to preserve the building and its contents. It can still be used for occasional services. Meanwhile its 15th century wood paneling and its unique brasses are safe, as are its ancient choirstalls and misericords, and its 15th century 'hour glass' pulpit.

And St. Mary the Virgin, Edlesborough is 'twinned' with St. Mary the Virgin, Eaton Bray.

Books Published by
THE BOOK CASTLE

CHANGES IN OUR LANDSCAPE: Aspects of Bedfordshire, Buckinghamshire and the Chilterns 1947-1992: Eric Meadows.
Over 350 photographs from the author's collection spanning nearly 50 years.
COUNTRYSIDE CYCLING IN BEDFORDSHIRE, BUCKINGHAMSHIRE AND HERTFORDSHIRE: Mick Payne.
Twenty rides on and off-road for all the family.
PUB WALKS FROM COUNTRY STATIONS: Bedfordshire and Hertfordshire: Clive Higgs. Fourteen circular country rambles, each starting and finishing at a railway station and incorporating a pub stop at a mid way point.
PUB WALKS FROM COUNTRY STATIONS: Buckinghamshire and Oxfordshire: Clive Higgs.
Circular rambles incorporating pub-stops.
LOCAL WALKS: South Bedfordshire and North Chilterns: Vaughan Basham.
Twenty-seven thematic circular walks.
LOCAL WALKS: North and Mid Bedfordshire: Vaughan Basham.
Twenty-five thematic circular walks.
FAMILY WALKS: Chilterns South: Nick Moon. Thirty 3 to 5 mile circular walks.
FAMILY WALKS: Chilterns North: Nick Moon. Thirty shorter circular walks.
CHILTERN WALKS:Hertfordshire,Bedfordshire and North Bucks: Nick Moon.
CHILTERN WALKS: Buckinghamshire: Nick Moon.
CHILTERN WALKS: Oxfordshire and West Buckinghamshire: Nick Moon.
A trilogy of circular walks, in association with the Chiltern Society. Each volume contains 30 circular walks.
OXFORDSHIRE WALKS: Oxford, the Cotswolds and the Cherwell Valley:
OXFORDSHIRE WALKS: Oxford, the Downs and the Thames Valley:
Both by Nick Moon.
Two volumes that complement Chiltern Walks: Oxfordshire, and complete coverage of the county, in association with the Oxford Fieldpaths Society. Thirty circular walks in each.
THE D'ARCY DALTON WAY: Nick Moon.
Long-distance footpath across the Oxfordshire Cotswolds and Thames Valley, with various circular walk suggestions.
THE CHILTERN WAY: Nick Moon.
A guide to the new 133 mile circular Long-Distance-Path through Bedfordshire, Buckinghamshire, Hertfordshire and Oxfordshire, as planned by the Chiltern Society.
JOURNEYS INTO BEDFORDSHIRE: Anthony Mackay.
Foreword by The Marquess of Tavistock, Woburn Abbey. A lavish book of over 150 evocative ink drawings.
JOURNEYS INTO BUCKINGHAMSHIRE: Anthony Mackay.
Superb line drawings plus background text: large format landscape gift book.
BUCKINGHAMSHIRE MURDERS: Len Woodley.
Nearly two centuries of nasty crimes.

WINGRAVE: A Rothschild Village in the Vale: Margaret and Ken Morley.
Thoroughly researched and copiously illustrated survey of the last 200 years in this lovely village between Aylesbury and Leighton Buzzard.
HISTORIC FIGURES IN THE BUCKINGHAMSHIRE LANDSCAPE:
John Houghton.
Major personalities and events that have shaped the county's past, including a special section on Bletchley Park.
TWICE UPON A TIME: John Houghton.
North Bucks short stories loosely based on fact.
SANCTITY AND SCANDAL IN BEDS AND BUCKS: John Houghton.
A miscellany of unholy people and events.
MANORS and MAYHEM, PAUPERS and PARSONS: Tales from Four Shires:Beds., Bucks., Herts. and Northants: John Houghton.
Little known historical snippets and stories.
MYTHS and WITCHES, PEOPLE and POLITICS: Tales from Four Shires: Bucks.,Beds., Herts. and Northants: John Houghton.
Anthology of strange, but true historical events.
FOLK: Characters and Events in the History of Bedfordshire and Northamptonshire: Vivienne Evans.
Anthology of people of yesteryear-arranged alphabetically by village or town.
JOHN BUNYAN: His Life and Times: Vivienne Evans.
Highly praised and readable account
THE RAILWAY AGE IN BEDFORDSHIRE: Fred Cockman.
Classic, illustrated account of early railway history.
A LASTING IMPRESSION: Michael Dundrow.
A boyhood evacuee recalls his years in the Chiltern village of Totternhoe near Dunstable.
GLEANINGS REVISITED: Nostalgic Thoughts of a Bedfordshire Farmer's Boy: E.W.O'Dell.
His own sketches and early photographs adorn this lively account of rural Bedfordshire in days gone by.
BEDFORDSHIRE'S YESTERYEARS Vol 2: The Rural Scene:
Brenda Fraser-Newstead.
Vivid first-hand accounts of country life two or three generations ago.
BEDFORDSHIRE'S YESTERYEARS Vol 3: Craftsmen and Tradespeople:
Brenda Fraser-Newstead.
Fascinating recollections over several generations practising many vanishing crafts and trades
BEDFORDSHIRE'S YESTERYEARS Vol 4: War Times and Civil Matters:
Brenda Fraser-Newstead.
Two World Wars, plus transport, law and order, etc.
PROUD HERITAGE: A Brief History of Dunstable, 1000-2000AD: Vivienne Evans.
Century by century account of the town's rich tradition and key events, many of national significance.

DUNSTABLE WITH THE PRIORY: 1100-1550: Vivienne Evans.
Dramatic growth of Henry 1's important new town around a major crossroads.
DUNSTABLE IN TRANSITION: 1550-1700: Vivienne Evans.
Wealth of original material as the town evolves without the Priory.
DUNSTABLE DECADE: THE EIGHTIES: A Collection of Photographs: Pat Lovering.
A souvenir book of nearly 300 pictures of people and events in the 1980s.
STREETS AHEAD: An Illustrated Guide to the Origins of Dunstable's Street Names: Richard Walden.
Fascinating text and captions to hundreds of photographs, past and present, throughout the town.
DUNSTABLE IN DETAIL: Nigel Benson.
A hundred of the town's buildings and features, plus town trail map.
OLD DUNSTABLE: Bill Twaddle.
A new edition of this collection of early photographs.
BOURNE and BRED: A Dunstable Boyhood Between the Wars: Colin Bourne.
An elegantly written, well illustrated book capturing the spirit of the town over fifty years ago.
OLD HOUGHTON: Pat Lovering.
Pictorial record capturing the changing appearances of Houghton Regis over the past 100 years.
ROYAL HOUGHTON: Pat Lovering.
Illustrated history of Houghton Regis from the earliest of times to the present.
THE STOPSLEY BOOK: James Dyer.
Definitive, detailed account of this historic area of Luton. 150 rare photographs.
THE STOPSLEY PICTURE BOOK: James Dyer.
New material and photographs make an ideal companion to The Stopsley Book.
PUBS and PINTS: The Story of Luton's Public Houses and Breweries: Stuart Smith.
The background to beer in the town, plus hundreds of photographs, old and new.
LUTON AT WAR 1
As compiled by the Luton News in 1947, a well illustrated thematic account.
THE CHANGING FACE OF LUTON: An Illustrated History: Stephen Bunker, Robin Holgate and Marian Nichols.
Luton's development from earliest times to the present busy, industrial town.
Illustrated in colour and mono.
WHERE THEY BURNT THE TOWN HALL DOWN: Luton, The First World War and the Peace Day Riots, July 1919: Dave Craddock.
Detailed analysis of a notorious incident.
THE MEN WHO WORE STRAW HELMETS: Policing Luton, 1840-1974: Tom Madigan.
Fine chronicled history, many rare photographs; author served in Luton Police for fifty years.

BETWEEN THE HILLS: The Story of Lilley, a Chiltern Village: Roy Pinnock.
A priceless piece of our heritage- the rural beauty remains but the customs and way of life described here have largely disappeared.
KENILWORTH SUNSET: A Luton Town Supporter's Journal: Tim Kingston.
Frank and funny account of football's ups and downs.
A HATTER GOES MAD!: Kristina Howells.
Luton Town footballers, officials and supporters talk to a female fan.
LEGACIES: Tales and Legends of Luton and the North Chilterns: Vic Lea.
Mysteries and stories based on fact, including Luton Town Football Club. Many photographs.
THREADS OF TIME: Shela Porter.
The life of a remarkable mother and businesswoman, spanning the entire century and based in Hitchin and (mainly) Bedford.
LEAFING THROUGH LITERATURE: Writers' Lives in Herts and Beds: David Carroll.
Illustrated short biographies of many famous authors and their connections with these counties.
A PILGRIMAGE IN HERTFORDSHIRE: H.M.Alderman.
Classic, between-the-wars tour round the county, embellished with line drawings.
THE VALE OF THE NIGHTINGALE: Molly Andrews.
Several generations of a family, lived against a Harpenden backdrop.
SUGAR MICE AND STICKLEBACKS: Childhood Memories of a Hertfordshire Lad: Harry Edwards.
Vivid evocation of gentle pre-war in an archetypal village, Hertingfordbury.
SWANS IN MY KITCHEN: Lis Dorer.
Story of a Swan Sanctuary near Hemel Hempstead.
THE HILL OF THE MARTYR: An Architectural History of St.Albans Abbey: Eileen Roberts.
Scholarly and readable chronological narrative history of Hertfordshire and Bedfordshire's famous cathedral. Fully illustrated with photographs and plans.
CHILTERN ARCHAEOLOGY: RECENT WORK:A Handbook for the Next Decade: edited by Robin Holgate.
The latest views, results and excavations by twenty-three leading archaeologists throughout the Chilterns.
THE TALL HITCHIN INSPECTOR'S CASEBOOK: A Victorian Crime Novel Based on Fact: Edgar Newman.   Worthies of the time encounter more archetypal villains.

SPECIALLY FOR CHILDREN
VILLA BELOW THE KNOLLS: A Story of Roman Britain: Michael Dundrow.
An exciting adventure for young John in Totternhoe and Dunstable two thousand years ago.
THE RAVENS: One Boy Against the Might of Rome: James Dyer.
On the Barton Hills and in the south-east of England as the men of the great fort of Ravensburgh (near Hexton) confront the invaders.

Books Distributed by THE BOOK CASTLE

All the above are available via any bookshop, or from the publisher and bookseller
**THE BOOK CASTLE , 12 Church Street Dunstable, Bedfordshire, LU5 4RU
Tel: (01582) 605670 Fax (01582) 662431 Email bc@book-castle.busclub.net**